"I'd use a metaphor to describ[  ] treasure! a deep well!), but th[  ] traordinarily creative and beautifully written, *You Are a Tree* is a soul-stirring companion to life in God's world that will enrich the spirit of all who read it. Highly recommended!"

David Zahl, director of Mockingbird Ministries
and author of *Low Anthropology*

"This delicious, deeply rooted sequence of meditations on some of the key metaphors in Scripture is a delight, at once refreshing and astringent. Joy Marie Clarkson takes familiar—sometimes overfamiliar—analogies from Scripture and poetry and helps us see and feel them as fresh, new, and thought-provoking."

Revd Dr Malcolm Guite

"As a writer and teacher of literature and composition, I love words. Joy's collection of essays here reads ultimately as a love letter to words and how God speaks His love for us through them. For that, I'm so glad Joy has shared her charming way with words with all of us."

Tsh Oxenreider, author of *Bitter & Sweet, Shadow & Light*,
and *At Home in the World*

"Joy Marie Clarkson's exploration of the way metaphors shape our imagination will make you fall in love with the beauty of language and be reminded of the marvelous mystery of life. Reading this book will make you more attentive to the glorious, strange experience of being made in the image of God."

Haley Stewart, author of *Jane Austen's Genius Guide to Life*
and editor for Word on Fire Spark

"In *You Are a Tree*, Joy Marie Clarkson combines the biblical motif of metaphor with insightful artistic allusions as she leads us into a rich conversation about the soul's relationship with God. And she does so with the keen intellect of a scholar and the winsomeness of a skilled communicator."

Brian Zahnd, author of *The Wood Between the Worlds*

"Gentle, wise, and thought-provoking, this lovely meditation on metaphor will help you think (and pray) more."

Elizabeth Oldfield, host of *The Sacred* podcast

# YOU ARE A TREE

## Books by Joy Marie Clarkson

*Aggressively Happy*

*You Are a Tree*

# YOU
# ARE
# A
# TREE

## AND OTHER
## METAPHORS TO NOURISH LIFE,
## THOUGHT, AND PRAYER

# JOY MARIE CLARKSON

BETHANYHOUSE

a division of Baker Publishing Group
Minneapolis, Minnesota

Published by Bethany House Publishers
Minneapolis, Minnesota
BethanyHouse.com

Bethany House Publishers is a division of
Baker Publishing Group, Grand Rapids, Michigan

Printed in the United States of America

ISBN 9780764238253 (paper)
ISBN 9780764242748 (casebound)
ISBN 9781493445141 (eBook)

Library of Congress Control Number: 2023045273

Published in association with The Bindery Agency, www.TheBinderyAgency.com

Baker Publishing Group publications use paper produced from sustainable forestry practices and post-consumer waste whenever possible.

24  25  26  27  28  29  30      7  6  5  4  3  2  1

To my father, Clay King Clarkson,
Who, through puns, play, poetry, and prose,
taught me the pleasure and power of language.

That person is like a tree planted
by streams of water,
which yields its fruit in season
and whose leaf does not wither—
whatever they do prospers.

Psalm 1:3

# CONTENTS

# INTRODUCTION

## Muddying the Waters

> Speaking of the plentiful imagery of the world . . .
>
> Billy Collins, "Litany," *Nine Horses*

I had moved house at least once a year for seven years straight. It is simply the way of life during higher education, the path I chose in my early twenties. When the short years of an undergraduate degree expire, one is sent into a seemingly endless game of musical chairs; if you're not moving for a new degree or a new short-term job, you're moving to find a cheaper place to live or a better roommate, or simply bending yourself to the will of campus housing. It became wearying, but as the years wore on, I began to strategize. In preparation for my move to each new domicile, I kept a few prized possessions, pictures, sentimental things, and valuable household items to be loaded into a singular cardboard box. I'd collected these objects in hopes that one day I'd have my own home, where they could be of use or gather dust on a decorative shelf. "Have nothing in your house which you do not know to be useful, or believe to be beautiful"[1] wrote William Morris, and I tried to follow his maxim. But each year as another June rolled around, a less idealistic proverb formed itself in my mind: have nothing in your apartment which you do not know to be disposable, or believe to be easily transported.

For me, the necessity of portability did not begin in college. If you were out to dinner with my mother and asked her where our family was from, she would grin and with a twinkle in her eye recite the (to me) familiar formula: "We've moved sixteen times, six times internationally" to the consternation of the listening party. Each of my siblings was born in a different state or country, and until my parents moved into our family home in Colorado, they had never stayed in one house for more than three years. The possibility that next year, next month even, I might need to move again has always been more than that to me; it is a probability, no, an inevitability. And so, when, during my studies, I settled into a flat for more than a year—twenty-seven months to be exact—it felt almost miraculous. But eventually my studies came to a close, and it was time to move again.

I sat on the stoop of my flat that breezy September morning, a shambolic mess of half-packed cardboard boxes within, and sighed. I was sad in a tired way. I had grown to like the overgrown garden our flat shared with the letting agency below: the pear trees that were supposedly grafted from medieval trees, the overburdened trellis of roses with limbs arched in blossomed exhaustion, the tree that produced six perfect red apples each fall (no more, sometimes less), even the tropical tree with large, waxy leaves that seemed not quite at home in this gusty Scottish climate. I looked on them with a mixed pleasure. I envied the impassive stability of these trees; they would go on sprouting, blossoming, changing colors with the seasons, not caring whether I stayed or left, lived or died. Oh, to be so stubborn in one's being and one's needs, so sure of one's literal place in the world.

*I am a potted plant*, I said to myself. *Always ready to be moved, never mingling my roots with those of my neighbors, a stranger to solid ground.*

This thought fell into my mind like a blunt object. Inside my house was a small potted plant that I had taken pains to keep alive during the final throes of completing my thesis, like a talisman of my own survival. I had been contemplating what to do with it when I left and considering throwing it away. It had taken on a wild, stringy appearance no matter how I groomed and clipped it, as though in protest against its modest pot, signaling to me that it wanted to get out and spread itself into welcoming soil. The metaphor continued to unravel itself within my knotted stomach. *Perhaps I am a plant that has grown too large for its pot, a plant that if it does not find real soil to set its roots in soon will become awkward and sad, limbs reaching pleadingly toward the sun at the window, wanting to feel the worms and wetness of early morning, but always kept outside of such experiences.* Lately, the sight of the plant had begun to inspire a plaintive despair in me; I had tried to plant indoor plants outside before, but they soon died, their roots shocked by the experience. Darkly, I thought to myself that perhaps I was the same. *Perhaps after all these years of life with portable roots, I was no longer capable of natural rootedness. Perhaps if you tried to plant me in a particular place, I would shrivel up and die, not ready for the exposure of pure obligation to a place.* I longed for a place to belong, to be entangled with, but felt in my bones incapable of such a thing.

## Like and Is

This is a book about paying attention—to our experiences, and to the words we use to describe them.

Looking out on that tangled abundance of garden and finding in it, or perhaps more precisely, finding in alienation from it, the words *I am a potted plant* gave me an immediate sensation of both pain and relief. My complicated feelings about my nomadic history had already begun to surface within me, but I hadn't named or parsed them. I could have tried to untangle the threads of disconsolation I found within myself: the longing for membership somewhere, for obligation even, the loneliness, the strange way the whole world being your oyster makes you feel cramped, and, perhaps above all, the weariness. But each of these feelings was buried, entwined, intermingled, related to each other. By carrying over the properties of the potted plant, this tangible, visible thing, to my own intangible anguish and invisible stirrings, I gave voice to something real and pressing. In the tangled mess of unruly foliage, trying so hard to be fruitful in inhospitable circumstances, I saw myself. It pained but also satisfied me. The intangible feeling within me had been given form.

This is the work a good metaphor can do in our lives. As human beings, we have these deep and unutterable experiences: loving someone deeply, our sense of calling, the mutating pain of family dysfunction, our conviction that something is wrong in the world, the fraught stirrings of our belief (and unbelief) in God, the transformative joy of having a child, the losses and disappointments we all encounter in life. These things live within us, they shape and direct our lives, and we find them difficult to speak about. There are other essential things that are difficult to talk about too—goodness, justice, wrongdoing, and in the quiet whisperings of all these things, God. These things elude us, shapeshifting and dissolving when we try to put them into words. And yet we feel a deep and insatiable desire to put these things into words, to speak about our experiences of the world and our ideas, to give these things shape so that we can look at them, talk about them, show them to other people so they can be witnessed, maybe even understood. Very often, when we are not able to speak about our experiences and ideas, to give them voice, they fester within us, growing infected or stale. On the opposite end of the spectrum, we may feel that a joy or a love is not complete if we cannot rejoice in it out loud, give it the honor it is due in the distinctly human language of praise.

Metaphors matter because they allow us to give a voice to those profound experiences and concepts that evade us, because giving voice to those things is satisfying, clarifying, honoring, and humane, and because the metaphors we choose and use direct our actions, our orientation in the world. That is what this book will explore by meditating on seven metaphors offered to us in the Christian and Hebrew

Scriptures. But I'm getting ahead of myself. We must begin with a simpler question.

What is a metaphor?

To answer this, we must keep in mind two important words: *like* and *is*. A simile is simple; it marks out the similarities between things: this is like that. The poet Robert Burns (or Bobby Burns as he's called in his native Scotland) has one of the most famous examples of a simile in love poetry. In one of his favorite love ballads he says the following about his beloved Scottish lassie:

> O, my luve's like a red, red rose
> That's newly sprung in June;
> O, my luve's like a Melodie
> That's sweetly played in tune.[2]

This is a simile. Burns observes similarities between his "luve" and a red, red rose, and later, a melody sweetly played in tune. What is happening here is a comparison, like with like. A rose has certain features—loveliness, pleasing fragrance, appeal—that his "luve" also has. They are like each other. A simile does the work for the reader, telling them "this is like that." I am *like* a potted plant.

The operative word in a metaphor is, well, *is*. Or sometimes *are*, when the grammar calls for it. Let us look to another love poem for an example of metaphor: "Litany" by Billy Collins. In this poem, Collins describes someone, whom I have always assumed to be a romantic partner, as various things. He declares with ontological authority that his beloved is the dew, the sun, the baker's apron. The lover (as I imagine him or her) is definitively *not* various other things: a breeze, a house of cards, and very definitely not the pine-scented air.[3] It's an endearing little poem, written with affection and playfulness, much less saccharine than the famous womanizer Bobby Burns' sappy words. And yet, in a way, Burns' words seem more believable. To say that your love is *like* a red rose, even *like* a melody; that makes sense. But what does it mean to say that your love *is* an apron, the sun, bread, dew, a flock of birds? How can we understand it?

Etymologically, *metaphor* literally means to "carry over" (*meta* "trans" + *pherein* "'to carry'"). (Let the reader understand and enjoy the irony of providing a *literal* definition of *metaphor*). The most famous definition of metaphor comes from Aristotle's *Poetics*, where he says, "Metaphor is the application of a strange term either transferred from the genus and applied to the species or from the species and applied to the genus, or from one species to another or else by analogy."[4] The technical word for this aspect of metaphor is *transference*. To put this more simply, a metaphor is when we use words to carry the properties that naturally (or rather, properly) belong to one thing over to another thing: I don't really have roots, but I carry them over to my experience in an attempt to understand it. The transference runs from the plant to me; roots are proper to plants.

Let us examine another metaphor: he is a real *wet blanket*. The subject of the metaphor is a person, and when we use this metaphor we are usually not describing the literal wetness of sweat or water, we are describing someone who makes things more somber, heavy, less enjoyable. We mean that someone isn't very much fun, that they *dampen the mood*.

With these words we draw qualities more proper to a wet blanket (they can cover things, they put out fires, they are cold and damp, they are uncomfortable and inhibit movements) to describe someone who covers a social situation with awkwardness, reduces fun, makes things less lively, just like a wet blanket weighs and dampens what it touches. But weighing down and dampening are properties usually more proper to a blanket than to a personality. This is because a "personality" is an elusive thing, something we imagine dwelling within someone, or an amalgamation of their interactions with the world and themselves. We can't capture a personality and put it in a jar. So instead, we carry the qualities of a wet blanket over to our experience of a boring person. Once we've found the metaphor we say, "Aha! Yes! That's just it."

But of course, a person is not a wet blanket, and Collins' lover is *not* a breeze in the orchard. A simile is content to notice the similarities between two things and leave it alone; "my luve's *like* a red, red rose," but love is not *actually* a red, red rose. A metaphor invites us to imagine that a boring person really *is* a wet blanket. And yet, there is a playful game in metaphors. They wink at us. And that's a part of the fun. The whispered word in a metaphor is *not*; you are (not) the goblet and the wine. He is (not) a wet blanket. I am (not really) a potted plant. Metaphors are as much about noncorrespondence as they are correspondence. They are, as Aristotle puts it, "the application of a strange term" onto a thing. This is why French philosopher Paul Ricoeur proposes what might be described as a tension theory of metaphor. The tension, in this case, is between a literal and metaphorical interpretation. In a metaphor, the literal meaning of the words is nonsense, so a metaphor requires an interpretation besides a literal interpretation to make sense of it.[5] In light of this, metaphor is a matter of tension within sentences rather than a substitution of one word for another. Metaphors fail or rupture, but these "failures" in themselves give us more room in which to discover what things are really like, to probe the similarities and dissimilarities in the objects of the metaphor. The pressure in a metaphor bursts open the thing we are trying to describe so we pay attention to the correspondent properties of the image and the thing described that we hadn't noticed before. But in noticing where the metaphor stops, we are also forced to pay closer attention to why the thing *isn't* actually what we describe it to be. Metaphors are the fruit of attention, but they ought to also make us pay closer attention so we are not deceived or confused by them.

## You Are (Not) a Machine

I described myself as a potted plant, but a more commonly used metaphor in everyday modern life is that of people as machines, or, more specifically, as computers. Perhaps you are doubtful. You think that you have never described yourself as a machine, or thought, *I am a computer.* But think of how we describe ourselves *processing* something like a hard drive whirring away, or how we tell a friend that we need to *update* each other about life events, like new software. We *adjust* to new circumstances like a car whose tires need to be rotated; people *push our buttons*; we need to *power down* so we can *recharge.* When we don't understand something, we might say it *does not compute.* When someone has been influenced to think or behave in a certain way, we say that they were *programmed to trust authority*. We might describe ourselves as a *slow processor*. This metaphor can even be a compliment: of someone who is particularly productive we often say *they are a machine*.

What are the qualities of a computer? A computer is a collection of parts that have a specific function and can be replaced. Computers are self-contained. One can expect a computer to behave in the same way every day (I certainly do!), to "need" the same things every day (a charger, a working outlet, enough space on a hard drive, software updates). Computers are intelligent and objective; they are not loyal to one user or another. When a computer breaks, really breaks (if you ran over it with a car or a virus took over its software), there's no real use in keeping it. It is expendable. How do these qualities carry over to humans in this metaphor? Humans, too, have many parts, and, if I may be so bold to say it, we are intelligent. But here, it begins to get muddy. If we are computers, then we should be able to expect the same thing of ourselves every day; if we are not behaving, performing, or producing at the same speed, something is wrong with us. If we are a computer, when one part of our life malfunctions we should be able to remove it and replace it with something better. If we are computers, we should be both intelligent and objective, making choices based on what will maximize our happiness and effectiveness. If we are computers, when we stop working, there is nothing to be done; we are no longer valuable and should be disposed of.

There are, of course, ways in which we are like a computer: we have limited energy, which we need to replenish, like a computer losing charge. Sometimes the experience of learning something feels like inputting data, and it takes some time to work its way through our view of the world, to *process*, that is. But many of these qualities do not apply to humans, at least without significant qualification. We are not self-contained; our environments affect us—the season, the quality of our relationships, how well we've slept, what we had for breakfast. Because of this, we do not produce the same thing every day. Our lives are not made up of discrete parts that can be replaced with a different version of the same piece when one breaks. We become deeply and irrationally attached to things; loyal sometimes even to people or places that would destroy us. If we have one romantic disappointment, we cannot simply pick another person and shove them into our lives like we're replacing a faulty battery. And for better or worse, though we are intelligent, we are almost never objective. Operating under this metaphor, we will often find ourselves stymied and exasperated by these fleshy bodies and pesky emotions that make their demands and insupportable decisions.

As a systematic metaphor for human flourishing, *humans are computers* is both incomplete and unforgiving. When we describe ourselves as computers, we tend to start treating ourselves as if we are, expecting of ourselves those things we can expect of a computer. There is a sharp edge to this metaphor, and a real danger. When we begin to think of ourselves as computers, we might subtly absorb the idea that what we are as a creature is primarily valuable for what we can produce. Ironically, we often buckle under the weight of this expectation, becoming less "productive" than we might have been if we acted like the ordinary creatures we are. The inadequacy of the metaphor is a danger beyond making us less productive: there is real peril in allowing ourselves to subtly accept the idea of our (or anyone else's) disposability, the value of human persons for their ability to "function" efficiently. Computers are brought into existence to perform a function; when they expire, they are no longer valuable. When we submit ourselves to the language of computers, we make ourselves commodities with expiration dates; we devalue all in us that is not productive and useful. In this metaphor there is no room for the immense value of, as e.e. cummings puts it, a "human merely being."[6] Computers are replaceable; human beings are not. But so many of the merciless cogs in our society seem to disagree. See? I did it again: machine language.

We are not as simple as machines: we do not function the same way every day. But this is not a bad thing. Our porousness, our arbitrary loyalties and attachments, are not a mere weakness. And we are much more resilient than computers. I have not yet succeeded in regrowing a limb, but I have survived things my computer couldn't dream of. It is not that human beings are a bad version of computers. The metaphor ultimately fails to grasp the needs and strengths of human beings because a machine, even a very advanced one like a computer, is for the most part much less sophisticated in design than the constantly morphing organism that is a human. We can do things computers can't yet even dream of. We can clot blood, write poetry, form romantic attachments, and cook spaghetti Bolognese all while being, according to human standards, fairly stupid.

The ways in which we "fail" to be a computer fall close to humankind's greatest strengths: loyalty, resilience, intuition, creativity.

The pervasiveness of this metaphor reveals two things to me. First of all, that the metaphors we use to describe ourselves and the world shape how we understand ourselves and how we act in the world. When we absorb this metaphor into our everyday imagination, it begins to shape our expectations of ourselves. When our productivity waxes and wanes, when our emotions and attachments get in the way, when simple solutions for our problems don't work, we can become exasperated with ourselves and cruel; *Why can't you just work? Produce? Get over it? This isn't rational! Why are you so dramatic and inefficient? Why are you so broken? What is the point of you?* Which leads me to the second thing it reveals: there are better and worse metaphors, metaphors that are closer or further from the truth, that possess greater or fewer similarities to the things they seek to describe. There are metaphors that can damage and exhaust and metaphors that relieve and revitalize, redirecting action toward health.

Ironically, the word *computer* did originally apply to human beings. Its earliest use (dating back to at least the seventeenth century) referred to someone who did mathematical computations: one who computed. This use continued well into the twentieth century, only coming to mean a machine that makes computations around the invention of the Turing machine. In a way, the word was a metaphor: it carried the properties of a person who did computations over to a machine. The direction of the metaphor got confused, and it stuck. This happens fairly often.

## God Is (Not) a Rock

A few years ago, I purchased a reprinting of a medieval bestiary from a used book shop. A bestiary, as its name suggests, is a compendium of beasts, a strange mixture of what we would now call science, poetry, and theology. In each entry, the author (likely a monk or priest) gives a brief description of an animal, ranging from rats to panthers to unicorns. The descriptions are a mixture of accurate facts— for instance, that panthers are hunters—with seemingly fanciful descriptions, like that panthers have multicolored coats and sweet-smelling breath to which all animals are drawn. These descriptions are paired with illuminated and colorful illustrations that lead the modern reader to conclude that author of the bestiary had probably never encountered a panther in real life; the panther, with its multicolored coat, breathes on many appreciative animals, who are blissfully lapping up his sweet breath. And if all this were not charming and surprising enough, almost every entry in the bestiary ends with the same formulation, which is something to the effect of "and the True Panther is our Lord Jesus Christ."

While writing this book, I have found myself feeling a bit like the author(s) of the bestiary. As I meditated on each metaphor, the imagery it evokes, the phenomena it explores, and the Scriptures associated with it, I often found myself landing in the same place: the True Light/Tree/Tower is our Lord Jesus Christ. Given what I've said so far about metaphor, this should lead us to ask a thorny question: isn't it dangerous to do this? In asking this question, we might look to Scripture and find that in the Christian and Jewish traditions, not only is it okay to speak about God in metaphor, it is done all the time. "The Lord is my rock" writes the psalmist (18:2), and a dozen other metaphors can be found throughout the pages of Scripture: God as a potter (Isaiah 64:8), a mother bear (Hosea 13:8), the sun (Psalm 84:11), a warrior (Exodus 15:3). And then there are Jesus' own self-identifications as various things, the so-called "I am's" of the Gospel of John: *I am the bread of life; I am the light of the world; I am the gate for the sheep; I am the good shepherd; I am the resurrection and the life; I am the way and the truth and the life; I am the true vine* (6:48; 8:12; 10:7, 11; 11:25; 14:6; 15:1).

That it is permissible to speak about God in this earthly, vivid, concrete language is abundantly evident; it is necessary even. But what happens when we do this? In using these metaphors are we not, as Aristotle puts it, applying "strange terms" to God? And what are we to do with the fact that we call the first person of the Trinity "Father"? Is that merely a metaphor? Are we imposing strange terms onto the very heart of the Godhead?

This is a question of property and transference; what qualities are proper to God? And which direction is the transference taking place? There is a passage in a book I love that, I think, puts this question into a striking and beautiful relief. The book is *Revelations of Divine Love* by the fourteenth-century Julian of Norwich, the first book written by a woman in English. She writes:

> The Mother's service is nearest, readiest, and surest: [nearest, for it is most of nature; readiest, for it is most of love; and surest] for it is most of truth. This office none might, nor could, nor ever should do to the full, but He alone.

27

We know that all our mothers' bearing is [bearing of] us to pain and to dying: and what is this but that our Very Mother, Jesus, He—All-Love—beareth us to joy and to endless living?—blessed may He be! Thus He sustaineth us within Himself in love; and travailed, unto the full time that He would suffer the sharpest throes and the most grievous pains that ever were or ever shall be; and died at the last. And when He had finished, and so borne us to bliss, yet might not all this make full content to His marvellous love; and that sheweth He in these high overpassing words of love: *If I might suffer more, I would suffer more.*[7]

Julian seems to be doing something similar to the scribes in the bestiary, excavating an experience to see Christ in it. Most of us find our language for love within the context of tangible human relationships. For some, our earliest and most profound experience of love might be from our mother. In *Revelations of Divine Love*, Julian of Norwich draws on the experience of mother love to understand Christ's self-giving love; this love is ready to sacrifice, to pour out, to do whatever the child needs. I find it striking that Julian seems to go beyond suggesting motherhood as an appropriate metaphor for the experience of God's love. Rather, she proposes that the properties of earthly motherhood are borrowed from and hallowed by the true motherhood of God. Beautiful, loving earthly motherhood draws its sap from the branches of the everlasting tree.

In her masterful meditation, Julian seems to switch the direction of transference; she suggests that motherhood is proper to God, not human beings. And for many readers, this makes us uncomfortable; it feels like we're taking a human experience and projecting it onto God. That people are less likely to feel this way about the language of Fatherhood could be simply because it is more prevalent in Scripture and in the Christian tradition. But is the metaphor fundamentally different? Is God *really* a father but only *metaphorically* a mother? What is proper to God? One solution to this problem is to never speak about God, or to speak only in negations, to say only what we cannot know about God. Even here, metaphor can help us, since hidden within it is always that "not": God is (not) a rock, God is (not) a mother bear. When we speak in metaphor, we are aware, on some level, that our words cannot contain the expansive and radiant nature of God, something that is less clear to us when we attempt to use "literal" language, when we might be tempted to think we really have said something successfully and finally about God, put some small attribute of God's in a box.

Another way to approach this would be to say that only those qualities of God that would be in God even *without* creation are proper to God. God would be "life" (self-animating) without creation, but He might not be a rock since God is not (in a traditional framework) material. And yet even this opens strange questions, doesn't it? Because all things are created by God and proceed from God. As Paul says, quoting the ancient poets, "in him we live and move and have our being" (Acts 17:28). The theologian Thomas Aquinas answers the question in this way:

> Our knowledge of God is derived from the perfections which flow from Him to creatures, which perfections are in God in a more eminent way than in creatures. . . . Our intellect apprehends them as they are in creatures, and as it

apprehends them it signifies them by names. Therefore as to the names applied to God—viz. the perfections which they signify, such as goodness, life and the like, and their mode of signification. . . . These names, they belong properly to God, and more properly than they belong to creatures, and are applied primarily to Him. But as regards their mode of signification, they do not properly and strictly apply to God; for their mode of signification applies to creatures.[8]

I have not settled on an answer to this question of how to speak about God other than to borrow the language Scripture has given me, but I wanted to put the question into your mind as you read this book. As you explore each metaphor in this book, ponder the question: does this excellence derive from God? Is God offering me a window into His excellencies by using a piece of His good creation? As we ask these questions, we brush the hem of the great tapestry of analogy that entangles many of these questions. But that is a question for another book. For now, let us return to trees.

## Traveling Trees

I am not the only potted plant. In centuries past, the odds were good that you would grow up, marry, and work within a short distance of the same place where you were born. Now it is less likely to be the case. Writing in response to the moral and economic desolations of World War II, Simone Weil drew on this metaphor in her book *The Need for Roots*, describing the modern condition as one of rootlessness, a lack of meaningful community, work, and belonging, a loss many of us feel in our souls. Some have tried to react to this sense of itinerancy constructively, by choosing a place to put down their roots for good. The notion is noble but comes with its own angst. It is very difficult to belong to a place, to not be able to escape it, to be bound to petty church politics, racist neighbors, the limitations of *this place*. And how does one choose a place? There is a loneliness of knowing that your rootedness is a chosen rootedness, not the inheritance of love and history. This was a pain I first put my finger on in the golden idealism that first comes with reading a Wendell Berry novel. After a period of wistful desire to take up farming and only use a typewriter, I began to feel a sassier question rising to my pen: it's all fine and good, Mr. Berry, but what if I have no ancestral farm? And, how far back do I have to look to discover the farm isn't so ancestral after all?

The feeling of rootlessness stretches much further back past our present predicament. One credible description of history is a long legacy of displacement; of winning and losing land, of conquering and being driven out, of building homes and having them destroyed, by war or time, greed, or boredom. Rootlessness is not merely a feature of the modern condition but also of the human condition.

I felt this keenly when I first read Saint Augustine's *Confessions*, where he touches this ancient wound in a surprisingly vivid way. The North African saint whose words and ideas have echoed down through the centuries described human nature as being characterized by a kind of restlessness. He famously writes in his *Confessions*, "We are restless until we find our rest in thee."[9]

Augustine was what we might call a third-culture kid— the son of a Christian North African mother and a pagan

Roman father—never quite fitting anywhere. Reading the story of his early life in *Confessions* is strikingly relatable to us sufferers of (post)modern malaise. As a young man he reinvented himself again and again. First, he fashioned himself as a hedonist and a social climber, intoxicated by romance and every pleasure that came his way. Made a bit sick by his own overindulgence, Augustine turned to a restrictive lifestyle, joining a gnostic cult with strict rules for living and high-minded ideas about the spiritual world. Finally, and perhaps most tragically, he fell in love, taking a lover with whom he had a child, and whom, by all accounts, he never gave up loving. In each act of his recounted life, there is a tragic sense of longing, unsatiated desire. When I read his fraught words, I can't help but feel that Augustine, too, was a potted plant, withering with desire.

But Augustine took a different metaphor as the interpretive key for his life: a journey, or, rather, an exile. Sarah Stewart-Kroeker writes, "Augustine's dominant image for the human life is *peregrinatio*, which signifies at once a journey to the homeland (a 'pilgrimage') and the condition of exile from the homeland."[10] All of life for Augustine was shaped both by this search for the homeland and the feeling of exile; he was a potted plant searching for welcoming soil. This feeling characterizes not only the ethos of his theology, but also the arc of his own personal narrative. In Augustine's story, I found resonances of my own: the desire for rest and rootedness mixed with the sense of exile and strain toward a place of belonging. Here, I began to find myself mixing metaphors. I am a potted plant; I am a pilgrim. The image it presented to me was awkward and funny, like Tolkien's glacially slow and meandering tree-people, the ents. What could flourishing look like for this mixed metaphorical life? How can one succeed as both a pilgrim and a tree? Of a promising person we say *they are going places*. We do not say that of a successful tree. A successful tree stays put. It has roots. It bears fruit.

Somewhere along the way, I discovered that this mixed metaphor is at the heart of one of the Bible's most famous passages: Psalm One. This is what it says:

> Blessed is the one
>> who does not walk in step with the wicked
> or stand in the way that sinners take
>> or sit in the company of mockers,
> but whose delight is in the law of the Lord,
>> and who meditates on his law day and night.
> That person is like a tree planted by streams of water,
>> which yields its fruit in season
> and whose leaf does not wither—
>> whatever they do prospers.
> Not so the wicked!
>> They are like chaff
> that the wind blows away.
> Therefore the wicked will not stand in the judgment,
>> nor sinners in the assembly of the righteous.
> For the Lord watches over the way of the righteous,
>> but the way of the wicked leads to destruction.

The blessed person walks, like a pilgrim (v. 1), but the blessed person is also like a tree (v. 3). At first the psalm begins as a simile, but it unfolds the likeness in metaphor; the righteous are not only like the tree, they *are* planted, yielding, prospering. At the heart of these two images is not only the (not) nature of metaphor but also some of the central tensions of what it is to be a human. We flourish in rootedness and fruitfulness, but that rootedness is always temporary, interrupted by death. And even in life we are driven by longings this world never seems capable of satisfying. By reflecting on the properties of trees and journeys, and carrying them over to the human condition, we might discover new ways of understanding ourselves. And even in the ruptures of the metaphors, those places where there is not correspondence, we might discover and articulate those ruptures and noncorrespondences in the human experience that cause us most discomfort and pain. In speaking about them, in giving them the form of images in our mind, we might find ourselves consoled, or drawn onward. For this reason, I have chosen to bookend these meditations with trees and journeys. These seemingly contradictory images invite us to consider what it is like to be human, to flourish, to live well in the contradictions of human nature, with the desire for eternity in the confines of mortality, roots in the ground and branches arching their weary arms toward their heavenly home.

## When Words Take Root

Life, like metaphors, is often not so much about resolving the tensions inherent within it, but learning to live within them, and even to let those tensions produce a pressure in which a valuable and coherent life might emerge. I have not solved the problem of my rootlessness, but gaining a language to speak about it has been helpful. The intervening years have been years of narrowing, of taking one step after another toward this garden and not another, the limitations within which a life can grow. Even now, I can feel the roots of my soul reaching down into the soil of the chosen inheritance of my life, searching and sometimes unsure and yet, somehow, already nourished.

In this book I will meditate on seven metaphors I find compelling in the Christian and Hebrew Scriptures: people are trees, wisdom is light, safety is a tower, love is a sickness, change is birth, sadness is heavy, and life is a journey. This is not an exhaustive list. There are many other metaphors in Scripture on which one could fruitfully meditate, but these are the ones that most piqued my curiosity and wonder. There are, one should note, many other metaphors in everyday life that are beautiful and rich and worth considering, but I chose to focus on metaphors in Scripture. This is for several reasons. First, there is a richness to these images because they have been meditated on, written about, painted, subverted, and reasserted for thousands of years. Their longevity seems to testify to their richness and adaptability. They certainly gave me much more material to work with.

But I also chose them as conversation partners and sometimes antidotes to some of the newer metaphors that have crept into our parlance: humans as machines, for instance, and almost everything (time, relationships, religion) as money. Not all the metaphors in our world are good ones, and I think that some of these metaphors have the potential to be very damaging. These metaphors possess some explanatory power, and I do not wish to reject them all, but they do perhaps merit some circumspection. Will they endure? I don't know, but reflecting on the ways they interact with those more ancient metaphors from Scripture and more primal metaphors allows us to think more critically and poetically about how the metaphors of the world are directing, and sometimes misdirecting, our lives. Reflecting on those ancient metaphors doesn't erase the more recent metaphors but adds a healthy biodiversity to our imaginative and linguistic resources.

To this end, at the conclusion of every chapter, I have included recommendations for further reading, works of art, music, and poetry that explore each metaphor, with an eye to enriching the metaphorical well from which we draw. As you read, always keep in mind the (not) element of metaphors, that metaphors can never completely describe the thing they are referencing, that, through this tension, they only break them open and invite further inspection and reflection so you may consider them patiently and fruitfully. I would encourage you to stick with these images, meditate on them, write about them. I believe these images can take root, grow in your mind over time, and eventually produce fruit. For, after all, as you will soon learn:

You are (not) a tree.

# PEOPLE
## ARE (NOT)
# TREES

They will be like a tree planted by the water that sends out its roots by the stream. It does not fear when heat comes; its leaves are always green. It has no worries in a year of drought and never fails to bear fruit.

Jeremiah 17:8

The tree of life my soul hath seen,
Laden with fruit and always green;
The trees of nature fruitless be,
Compared with Christ the apple tree.
"Jesus Christ the Apple Tree,"
Eighteenth-Century Carol

called the house I lived in after my studies the "Tower." I wanted to live in a house rather than an apartment as a small concession to my desire for rest and recovery after that long season of uprootedness, exhaustion, and intensity. The house was old and creaky, and I would learn that I shared the space with a friendly commune of rats, but it was cozy. I called it the Tower because my bedroom was on the second story of a part of the building that had an octagonal shape. My bed was pushed back against one of the walls and surrounded by large windows looking out onto the overgrown woods of a nearby college. I loved that room. It felt safe, secure, and impenetrable (except to the cat who would climb in the second-story window in the middle of the night while I was asleep and terrorize me). I called the room my "nest" because the view out to the woods made me feel as if I were perched amidst the trees, almost a part of them myself. It gave me a front-row view of the seasons having their way with the branches and leaves of the unwieldy wood. I sat in my bed with a cup of tea in the mornings, finding solace in the effortless transformation that took place around me over my months in the Tower. In particular, I loved the cherry tree.

When I arrived in November, the cherry tree was bare, stripped of its leaves; its branches shot straight up into the sky in shameless, slender nakedness. It struck me as unpromising; how could its delicate limbs possibly withstand the blustery British winter? But when the first hint of spring came to breathe life into February, defiant little green knots appeared seemingly from one day to the next on the spindly branches. And when March came, and with it more bitter cold and resistance to warmth, a further miracle occurred: blossoms. The whole tree clothed itself in papery petals of a gentle rose white. It was resplendent even as winter persisted in recalcitrance. Would you believe me if I told you that at night it seemed to glow? I have pictures I could show you if you doubt me. This miracle lasted for a month before giving way to the more ordinary apocalypse of tender green leaves in May and the deeper shade of green that is the clothing of summer. As I came to the end of my time in the Tower, the cherry tree modestly began to shed its leaves again, even though they had never conceded to turn a proper yellow. When I left, the branches stretched smooth and leafless again into the sky, ready for the inevitable but unbelievable spectacle of its evolutions to begin once more.

I witnessed in my cherry tree the elegance of a living creature in perfect synchrony with the seasons. In its full and beautiful branches I saw a vision of what I could be were I to flourish, really flourish, in life. As the tree gained strength and vitality in the warming months of spring, I saw a mirrored replenishment of my own strength as that gentle year restored the weariness that had built up over years in me.

In my tree, I saw a vivid and theatrical display of flourishing, the kind of flourishing that perhaps the psalmist had in mind when he wrote these words:

> That person is like a tree planted by streams of water,
>   which yields its fruit in season
> and whose leaf does not wither—
>   whatever they do prospers.
>
> Psalm 1:3

We see ourselves in trees. We feel they are kindred, as though they have some sympathy with us. From where does this affinity spring? How deep are its roots? What might trees have to teach us about what it means to be human?

## Ancient Witnesses

Trees stretch their branches over almost every page of Scripture. It is difficult to find more than a page or two together that neglect to mention trees, whether it be reference to a tree, or words related to trees such as *fruit, branch, root, forest, vine, leaf,* or to the specific trees that have their parts to play in the drama of Scripture: *palm, cypress, ash, olive, oak, fig,* and more.

Many of the most significant moments in the Bible take place in the presence of trees. Eve eats from the tree of the knowledge of good and evil, resulting in humankind's expulsion from Eden (Genesis 3); Noah is given an olive branch as a sign of God's clemency and faithfulness (Genesis 8:11); Abraham is sitting under the oaks of Mamre when the mysterious visitors (thought, in many traditions to be the Trinity) come to visit (Genesis 18), and later he nearly sacrifices Isaac over a pile of wood (Genesis 22); Moses receives his commission from God as he stands barefoot in front of the burning bush (Exodus 3), which in Hebrew is simply another word for tree.

In these moments, trees stand as silent witnesses to the drama of humankind's relationship with God: moments of decision and desperation, of faithfulness and sin, of passing, or failing to pass, the tests of life. And this is a theme that has continued throughout the long history of imagery and poetry. In a poem etched into the sides of an eighth-century Celtic cross, an Anglo-Saxon writer imagines a tree witnessing the most significant moment of all: the crucifixion. The poem tells the story of the crucifixion from the perspective of the "rood" (cross) on which Christ died:

> They jeered us both, we two together. I was all
> spattered with blood,
> Drawn from this man's side as he had sent his spirit on.
> Much have I endured upon that hill
> of wrathful dooms. I saw the God of armies
> sorely stretched. Shadow had
> covered with clouds the ruler's corpse,
> [that once] shimmered with light. A shadow spread,
> pale under the clouds. All creation wept,
> Lamented the fall of the king. Christ was on the Rood.
> Nevertheless, they promptly came from afar
> To that prince. I beheld it all.[1]

*I beheld it all.* In this poem, the rood or cross itself (which many passages of Scripture describe simply as a "tree," e.g.,

Acts 5:30 ESV) is both witness and participant in the passion of Christ. It feels appropriate to speak of trees as witnesses. Their lives last longer than ours. They seem, somehow, to belong both to history and to the present.

The United States Library of Congress keeps a record of "Witness Trees," trees that have "seen" historic events in the history of the country. There is the Burnside Sycamore, which is said to have witnessed some of the bloodiest battles of the Civil War. Or the Oklahoma City Survivor, an American elm that survived the deadly blast of the Oklahoma City Bombing. The tree absorbed some of the blast from the 4,000-pound bomb. It was originally to be chopped down and investigated for the bits of the bomb that were thought to be hung in its branches and lodged in its trunk, but investigators were able to retrieve the evidence without cutting it down. The survivors and their families requested that it stand as a witness and a testimony of hope as a part of the bombing memorial. The official website describes the tree in these words: "The Survivor Tree, an American elm, bore witness to the violence of April 19, 1995, and withstood the full force of the attack."[2]

But it is not merely that we think of trees as witnesses; we also feel that they stand in solidarity with us, that they listen and are sympathetic to us, even though they do not speak. And, indeed, there is a comfort in the fact that trees do not speak. We have the sense that much has transpired under their watchful gaze, and yet they keep it to themselves. There is a comfort in a witness who keeps their counsel. Trees keep secrets. Wong Kar-Wai's melancholy film *In the Mood for Love* tells the story of two abandoned spouses caught in the anguish of what, it seems, can never be said.

Near the conclusion, years removed from the dissolution of his marriage, Mr. Chow says, "In the old days, if someone had a secret they didn't want to share . . . they went up a mountain, found a tree, carved a hole in it, and whispered the secret into the hole. Then they covered it with mud. And leave the secret there forever."[3] Mr. Chow travels to a temple in Cambodia, where he whispers his secrets into a small hole in the trunk-like pillars of the temple before filling it with moss and dirt. It is in this quiet ritual that the viewers experience the first hint of consolation for Mr. Chow.

Between trees and people, then, there is this old coalition. They watch us as we go about our tragic and joyful human doings. But it is not only that trees witness us, or even have sympathy for us. We also feel that trees are like us. The psalmist looks to our old friends the trees not merely for witnessing or keeping our secrets, but for presenting a portrait of what it looks like to thrive as a human being. And in their leafy arms he sees an answer: trees are *planted by streams of living water* and they *bear much fruit*.

## That Person Is Like a Tree Planted . . .

That trees are *planted* reminds us that trees have roots. Rootedness is one of the ways we intuitively describe the kind of stability that leads to flourishing and the kind of instability that leaves us dry, parched, and desperate. We speak of *upheaval* (like soil overturned in a barren field), of feeling *uprooted* due to drastic change, or even *unrooted*, like an astronaut suspended in space with no cord attached to the spaceship, floating gently into nothingness. The righteous man is like a *tree planted*, but the wicked are like *chaff*

43

*that the wind blows away* (Psalm 1:4). Roots offer literal security, grounding, openness to nourishment.

But roots remind us of something else too. Much of what comprises a tree is not visible. Roots tend to spread at least two to three times as wide as the canopy of a tree—sometimes much more. This means that when you look at the widest part of the top of a tree, the roots spread out two to three times past the radius of its branches; under good conditions, a tree with a ten-foot radius of branches will send its roots out twenty to thirty feet in any direction. The same is true of human beings.

What we see of the tree or of a person emerges from many things we cannot see. There is a hiddenness to trees that we find also in people. When you see someone walking around, working, and navigating relationships, you see a mystery formed by history, loves, movies watched, comic books enjoyed, and embarrassing moments they have done their best to forget. These hidden roots spread out in their being far further than you can imagine.

And so, too, do your roots. Histories, memories, desires, and connections run through the veins of each individual, shaping how they act and move in the world. Like a tree whose strong trunk emerges from the earth, erect and symmetrical, beneath the surface of who they are is a much more complicated system of tangled roots that made them grow the way they have, obstacles they've had to grow around, insufficient soil that has given some of their leaves an anemic look, depths of love that make them sturdy in the strongest gale though they may look delicate.

Like a tree, much of who we are goes unseen not only to onlookers but even to ourselves. In Augustine's *Confessions* he tells the story of his own life, carefully excavating experiences and memories in an effort to understand himself, the world, and God, to *arrive* at something like the truth. Often cited as the first autobiography, the book does not always read like a straightforward narrative; it meanders, and repeats, and gets lost. Theologian and former Archbishop of Canterbury Rowan Williams argues that this is not a bug of *Confessions*, but a feature of Augustine's approach. Williams writes that for Augustine,

> In a crucial sense . . . memory is what I am. The puzzle is that so much of what I am is absent from conscious awareness. To acknowledge the role of memory is to recognize that "I" am not a simple history to be unveiled and displayed for inspection, nor a self-transparent reasoning subject. . . . To be an intelligence in time is to be inescapably unfinished, consistently in search.[4]

My "self" is by its very nature mostly forgotten, buried under ten thousand days I can't remember. In a profound little play on words, Henry Jamison sings of the thousands of decisions that have made him who he is, concluding with self-effacing honesty, "I can't remember now; I forget myself."[5] Who I am is planted in the soil of the past and of forgetfulness.

That this should be the case is not necessarily a bad thing. The depth psychologists of the twentieth century went mad for this stuff, but there is a practical and commonsensical element to it, I think, beyond unlikely speculations about one's psychosexual development. Make what you will of the confident categorizations of Jung or Freud and their elaborate theories of repression, it seems true to me that forgetfulness can be a mercy. It isn't always healthy or helpful to dig up every root and try to trace its end in our childhood. We cannot bear all the bad things that happen to us all the time. It would disturb the well-being of a tree to constantly disinter the roots it had spent so many winters digging deep to establish.

Recognizing our planted-ness, however, allows us to approach ourselves and others with mystery, mercy, and patience. Mystery because it prevents us from assuming that we can understand and judge how someone came to be who they are and invites us to approach one another with an air of wonder—however tangled their roots may be, they have emerged here, standing tall. It encourages us to approach others with mercy since much of what forms our roots is not in our direct control; we did not get to choose which corner (or pot) of the world we'd be planted in, what family of trees our roots would be entangled with, what moles would make a home in the caverns of our root systems. And it allows us to approach ourselves and others with patience. While we might imagine roots as the physical manifestation of the past, fossilized fingers holding on to what has been, this is simply not the case. Trees are living things, and as long as they live, their roots are changing and growing. Deep, slow growth may be happening where we cannot see.

Sometimes, though, acknowledging the mystery of our plantedness can lead to a sense of loneliness. I have sometimes found myself dramatically thinking how hard it is to be known. We are each these microcosms, worlds unto ourselves, depths hidden away from even the very attentive eye. But this is not how roots work. In *The Hidden Life of Trees*, German forester Peter Wohlleben tells the story of scraping the moss away from an old and seemingly dead stump only to find a shock of green, indicating chlorophyll was still present in the tree, a sure sign of life. How could this stump, no longer capable of photosynthesis, still be alive? What had happened, he discovered, was that the neighboring trees had been feeding the roots of the stump, keeping it alive. And apparently this is not uncommon. Trees help each other, keeping one another alive even in extreme situations:

> A tree is not a forest. On its own, a tree cannot establish a consistent local climate. It is at the mercy of wind and weather. But together, many trees create an ecosystem that moderates extremes of heat and cold, stores a great deal of water, and generates a great deal of humidity. And in this protected environment, trees can live to be very old. To get to this point, the community [of trees] must remain intact no matter what. If every tree were looking out only for itself, then quite a few of them would never reach old age. Regular fatalities would result in many large gaps in the tree canopy, which would make it easier for storms to get inside the forest and uproot more trees. The heat of summer would reach the forest floor and dry it out. Every tree would suffer.
>
> Every tree, therefore, is valuable to the community and worth keeping around for as long as possible. And that is why even sick individuals are supported and nourished until they recover.[6]

We are mysteries, but in the depths of our roots is entwinement, with other histories and destinies. We are kept alive by the hidden depths of other people, not merely out of pity, but necessity. We need each other in mysterious, incalculable ways. We are connected by more than we know.

## By Streams of Water . . .

The blessed person is not only *planted*, but *planted by streams of water*. This phrase speaks to us of the sources of nourishment that a tree requires to flourish. Trees are complex organisms that require many aspects of their environment to align for them to thrive. In our elementary school science classes we all learned about photosynthesis, the way trees (and other plants) use sunlight, water, and carbon dioxide to generate the oxygen we all breathe and the sugar that fills their veins. No wonder we feel there is a solidarity between people and trees; trees give us the ingredients we need for a deep and healthy breath, the oxygen that fills our lungs and makes life on earth. Our lungs are filled with the exhale of trees.

But there is something in the process that also ought to remind us of ourselves: flourishing requires many good conditions, many different forms of nourishment. Photosynthesis (which is not the only process necessary to the life of a tree) requires sources of both sunlight and water. Trees need a large enough space for their roots to spread wide for sturdiness and to draw nutrients from the soil and not to cover each other's access to the sun in shadow. A tree needs sun, water, rich soil, and the involvement of creatures and insects hard at work to thrive. Every part of the tree affects the others; its access to sunlight affects the health of its roots, and the water its roots touch affects the

leaves. Trees are not the same every day. They are constantly adapting, changing, reaching—a perpetual feedback
loop, adjusting to the season, the weather, even the time
of day.

Once, during a period of exasperating insomnia, I
watched a nature documentary, hoping the dulcet tones of
David Attenborough might put me to sleep. I was, at the
time, frustrated with myself. It was a demanding era for me,
requiring a great deal of personal discipline to complete my
studies and carry on doing all the things that I needed to do
to pay my bills and appear as a rational member of society.
Each day, I had the same relentless routine of studying,
working, eating, cleaning, and preparing to do it all again.
And despite my best efforts, my pace of writing was glacial
and my body was constantly in some kind of rebellion—I
caught cold after cold and fell prey to migraines until I felt
quite literally dysfunctional: unable to function, to produce.
My insomnia was merely the final stone in an avalanche of
stress tumbling down the hill of my life.

David Attenborough was talking about palm oil trees.
Unlike me, apparently palm oil trees are very productive
and make a lot of money. This was probably not the impression David Attenborough wished me to take away from
the program, but I did feel slightly envious of the incredibly
productive trees. Farmers created the conditions for this
productivity by stripping away the many other seemingly
useless plants from the jungle, planting endless, orderly
lines of palm—and only palm—trees. What Attenborough
did wish me to catch, though, was that this process led to
the diminishment of the area surrounding the palm oil trees.
The relentless orientation toward producing palm oil began

to diminish the biologically rich resources that oriented the trees toward such productivity to begin with.

When Attenborough began to wax eloquent about the eating and pooping habits of a certain species of ape, I had a moment of clarity about the human condition. He spoke about how it takes years for them to teach their young what to eat, and that over the years, as they swing from tree to tree, eating and feeding their young, the excrement they leave behind plants seeds across the jungle, offering both fertilizer and a self-perpetuating system of biodiversity. This, suggested Attenborough, is the way of things: the chaos of the rainforest is the source of its life. Much of what appears useless, time-consuming, and unproductive is key to its survival. Thus, while the extreme order imposed by the farmers made an abundance of one kind of crop, it began to destroy everything else in its orderly path.

As I watched, I began to realize that I was thinking of myself like a palm oil tree. I was oriented around one purpose: to produce, produce, produce. I had cut and cleared the field of my life, vacating all that was not useful, all that did not directly contribute to the sustainment of my own existence and the productivity of my work. And as a result, the forest of my life was yielding less and less fruit. The world we live in has told us to make ourselves like palm oil trees, fit for producing and capitalizing. We leave little room in our lives for the wild and weedy flower of love or the unhurried snacking and pooping ape of curiosity to reside. And the irony of this, of course, is that we often make ourselves much less "productive" in the process by depriving ourselves of those secret and incalculable forms of nourishment. I resolved to reincorporate some of the frivolous sources of pleasure I had abandoned, which I suspected had somehow secretly fertilized my capacity for creativity, like the meandering and pooping ape. I resolved also to eat more leafy greens. I became sleepy. I never finished the documentary (apologies, Sir Attenborough), but my migraines became less frequent.

Each day, a tree needs something slightly different: sunlight, shade, water, nutrients in the soil, the reprieve of winter, springtime bees to fertilize its flowers, birds to pluck fruit so its branches won't break. A flourishing human life is the same. A good life is not made up of a few discrete ingredients, but of diffuse influences and sources of nourishment that cultivate a conducive context for fruitfulness. Some commentators believe that the phrase "planted by streams of water" refers to an irrigated garden, a place intentionally crafted to nourish trees. This suggests that the flourishing tree is flourishing not by happenstance or luck, but because of the careful, loving intention of a gardener who made the conditions good for the tree (and indeed, for all of the trees) to thrive. Perhaps, then, if we want to thrive, we must think of ourselves not only as the tree planted by streams of water, but as gardeners who intentionally make an environment conducive to fruitfulness. That we should do so is fitting, given that the first vision we are given of humankind is of two people set in a garden to tend it.

### Yields Its Fruit in Season . . .

It is interesting to meditate on the word *produce*. It is one of those odd words in English that can be both a noun and a verb. In its verb form, I can say that I will *produce* a manuscript by Easter of next year. In its noun form, I can say that I will feast on the *produce* of last year's apple harvest. In the battle of metaphors describing human beings, part of the disconnect between computers and trees is that computers can, generally speaking, *produce* the same things every day. Trees cannot. They have seasons, and even the healthiest, most fruitful tree will, the psalmist writes, *yield its fruit in season.*

This is one of the things humans and trees share together: they are both seasonal creatures, in both their macro and micro evolutions, their circles and their lines. There is the circle of each year: spring, summer, autumn, winter, and spring again, and there is the line of the passing of the years, of seasons piled on top of each other. A tree begins as a sprout, and then a sapling, and then a mature, fruit-bearing tree. Humans are the same, beginning as a baby, and then a toddler, a child, a young adult, an adult.

With each of these seasons come limitations. When it is winter, a tree usually cannot bear fruit, but this limitation is not a flaw; without the rest of winter, trees become exhausted and stop bearing fruit. And so each season comes with an abundance of possibility as well; in the autumn a tree can be beautifully heavy with fruit.

Humans, too, live in this world with seasons and are affected by them; we do not shed our leaves, but we go outside less, we sleep differently. And we too mature like a tree, not over the space of weeks or months like a puppy, but over years, decades even. And these circles are also played out in small circles of each day with its midnight darkness, rising sun, its noontimes, and its setting sun. With each of these stages and with each of these seasons we are limited or set free; in the dark I am limited in the amount of work I can do, but I am free to sleep because other people are also limited in the mischief they can get up to, and so I am less afraid.

However, due to the ingenuity of mankind, some of the limitations of seasons have become less pronounced. We have lightbulbs now, and central heating systems. Perhaps we might observe that they are not so different from candles and hearths, with the exception that they manage not only to mitigate the discomfort of darkness or cold (as candles and hearths do), but to nearly eradicate them, so that night is not so different from day, and winter from summer. We know they are, but the excuse is not as strong; why not stay up and work until midnight if we can? I am not one to bemoan technological advances; I am thankful for warm houses and the ability to write this book without the assistance of an amanuensis. But these useful technologies can sometimes prevent us from resting in the seasons.

Understanding ourselves as trees opens up possibilities for how we think about fruitfulness. For one thing, it removes the expectation of absolute uniformity, both in what we produce and how we produce it. Did you know that in a good year a fig tree can produce three crops? Contrary to this, if an apple tree bears too much fruit (and there is such a thing as too much!) it may only produce a crop every other year. I think we all want to be fig trees producing one crop, and then another, and then another. But if we are more like an apple tree, we'll push too hard on the one crop and be depleted when the next fruiting season comes around. Each tree is different, producing different fruits in different timelines. Each tree, like each happy person, yields their fruit *in season*. You can't be in a different season by trying harder. Each season has its gift and purpose; the nakedness of branches in winter prepares them for their glorious clothing of petals in spring.

When we see ourselves as trees we can accept the varying seasons of life, and even trust in their beneficial work. The psalmist does not say that the righteous man bears fruit *all the time*. Sometimes it can be frightening when it feels like our effort or prayer hasn't borne fruit. But remembering *you are a tree* can relieve some of this anxiety by reminding us that even wintery seasons (as long as they feel) may be a time when our roots are growing deep and may precede the decadent glory of spring. This perspective encourages us to pay attention to what is happening in our lives, what season we are in. Trees are constantly adjusting to the weather, the sun, the nutrients in the soil, the activity of bugs and animals. This invites us to adopt a posture of agency in those waiting and wintery seasons; you need not only weather the storm, but also figure out what you need in this season to ready yourself for the next. Do you need to draw strength from the other trees in the forest around you? Do your roots need to grow deeper? In this, meditation on the metaphor of trees can offer some hope: seasons come again and again. Just because you had an early frost in life does not mean you will not bear fruit again. Just because you feel stripped down by life does not mean you will not flower again. You are not a machine, useless when one (or many!) of its parts expire; you are a miraculous and beloved creation, with more resilience pulsing through your roots than you know.

## The True Vinedresser

The cherry tree outside my window gently tutored me in being human. As I watched its seasonal transformation, I was reminded of the way time accomplishes so much that mere effort cannot. In its barren branches, I saw my own long years of wondering what it was all for, hoping that my daily digging deep into the ground of my life meant something. And as I watched the little fists of green appear on the branches in preparation for foliage, I found within myself a tightly wound hope, ready to unfold and embrace a season of new beginnings. Watching the trees reminds us of how much of our lives is given rather than self-made, how much of fruitfulness is waiting and receiving.

But this can also bring to mind a tightness of concern growing in our chests: what if you or I have simply missed our springtime? Or a terrible storm has blown off your branches and bent you low so that you feel like a lifeless stump? What if you never bear fruit? Near the end of John's Gospel, when Jesus is preparing to go to His death, He says this to His disciples: "I am the vine; you are the branches. If you remain in me and I in you, you will bear much fruit; apart from me you can do nothing. If you do not remain in me, you are like a branch that is thrown away and withers" (John 15:5–6). Jesus seems to pick up on the imagery of Psalm 1, not only in His promise that abiding in Him will produce much fruit, but also in the promise that with Christ we *will not wither*. Christ is the source of nourishment from which our roots draw their strength, the *streams of water*, the tree that keeps the stump alive. But Christ is also the gardener who tends to the trees, pruning their branches. Earlier in the chapter, Jesus says, "I am the true vine, and my Father is the gardener" (John 15:1). Remembering that Christ is the true vine, and God the gardener can give us a peace and an active trust that we are not solely responsible for bringing about our own fruitfulness. Fruit is a gift of God's gentle love and care in our lives, not a reward for effort.

This is a difficult thing to trust. When I am a mystery to myself, it is difficult to imagine how the *living waters* might be nourishing my hidden roots, and it seems impossible to believe that *this season of barrenness* could ever end. But this is the mystery of being a tree: we cannot see our roots, we cannot provide our own nourishment, we are subject to seasons both fruitful and barren. But I find in me a seed of hope planted by the God of the garden, the God who looked for humankind "in the cool of the day" (Genesis 3:8); the God who plants the trees of the righteous by streams of living water (Psalm 1); the God who makes a shoot come out of the root of Jesse (Isaiah 11:1); who is the true Vine (John 15); who, in His first appearance after the resurrection, was mistaken for a gardener (John 20). All I need to do is to be a tree.

## LIVING, THINKING, PRAYING

> I pray that you, being rooted and established in love, may
> have power, together with all the Lord's holy people, to grasp
> how wide and long and high and deep is the love of Christ,
> and to know this love that surpasses knowledge—that you
> may be filled to the measure of all the fullness of God.
>
> Ephesians 3:17–19

## █ LIVING METAPHORS

Pick a tree that you have an occasion to see every day, be it out your window, on your commute to work, or in your garden. Keep track of its changes throughout the year: take a picture of it at the same time every day or write your observations in a notebook. Observe how it responds to the seasons and weather, its subtle changes from day to day, week to week, season to season. If you are a tree, in what season do you find yourself? From what waters and whose roots do you draw nourishment? What fruit has begun to grow in your life? What in your life needs more time?

## █ THINKING AND PRAYING

Painting: "The Hay Wain" (1821) by John Constable
Film: Little Forest (2018) by Yim Soon-rye
Image/Text: "The Tree of Life" by Bonaventura, British Library
Song: "Land Sailor" by Vienna Teng
Poem: "When Autumn Came," Faiz Ahmed Faiz
Podcast: "Tree of Life," The Bible Project

In this collection of images, music, and stories, we are given many different ways to think about the metaphor of people as trees. Constable's painting displays the lush beauty of a well-nourished copse of trees, a vivid picture of what is possible when a person is in a nourishing environment. The image invites us to consider what leads to the lush landscape—good soil, refreshed by a body of water, likely cultivated by a good steward. It is a picture to us of flourishing as a mixture of nature and nourishment, environment and effort.

*Little Forest* shows the fruits of such a conducive and nourishing environment in a person. The film follows Hye-won after she abruptly leaves her job in the impersonal city through the course of an entire year in a rural village. It moves gently and contemplatively through each season, dwelling on verdant landscapes and the intimate preparation of food gathered from the surrounding village in each season. The film quietly explores the protagonist's complicated relationship with her mother and her confusion over what she wants out of life. These questions are not answered but left to ripen over the changing seasons during the film, nourished by good food, time, sleep, and the companionship of Hye-won's friends.

Medieval thinkers loved to meditate on the tree of life, often connecting it in writings and images with the cross of Christ. In an elaborate mnemonic, the thirteenth-century Spanish bishop Bonaventure imagines the life of Jesus as a tree. Each event of Christ's life (his birth, baptism, passion, etc.) is represented by a piece of fruit offering itself as nourishment for his readers. This way of thinking of a life is interesting: events, trials, and important moments that may not be pleasant when they occur can become sweet and sustaining to us when allowed to ripen over time and with reflection.

In "Land Sailor," Vienna Teng explores the ways technology makes it so that we do not have to experience the seasons. She speaks of being able to buy a strawberry in the depths of winter, an experience previously only available to the richest of royals. She casts the possibilities of technology in the language of myth, seeing the gains of technology like a kind of exchange with the gods that might come at the cost of one's soul.

Pakastani poet Faiz Ahmed Faiz turns back to nature, seeing Christ's passion in the stripping of the trees during autumn. In his visceral descriptions of the cold violence of winter, the reader hears echoes of their own seasons of being stripped back and feeling barren. Near the end, the poem turns into a prayer asking that God will bless the trees with resurrection.

When you listen to the excellent series "Tree of Life" from The Bible Project, you will be amazed at the ubiquity of trees all throughout the Hebrew and Christian Scriptures, the deep symbolism in their branches, and the ways in which they evoke the saving work of Christ.

# WISDOM
## IS (NOT)
# LIGHT

Whoever walks in the dark does not know where they are going.

John 12:35

The Truth must dazzle gradually
Or every man be blind.

Emily Dickinson, "Tell all the truth
but tell it slant (1263)"

The darkness of four in the morning is darker than the darkness of midnight. Of this, I am reasonably convinced, and I have the common wisdom of idioms like "It's always darkest before the dawn" to back me up. I think perhaps this is because the world is more thoroughly asleep then; while a few windows may glow with midnight oil, even the most incurable of night owls have usually gone to their nest by four in the morning. Everything is still and cold in an achy way, the warmth of the previous day having dissipated overnight. It seems like anything could happen at four in the morning. And every single day something glorious and yet quotidian does happen: the sun rises over our world, *illuminating* and *enlightening* everything.

What does light do to a landscape? At first it is perceptible merely as a faint glow that washes over a shore of darkness, gradually offering to our vision the soft shapes of hills and housetops, and then, slowly but surely, the outlines of windows and chimneys. Seemingly in response to the call of the morning light, lamps begin to flicker on in kitchens and bathrooms, a visual work song of call and response into the industry of the day. In one sense all the light does is reveal; the land slept unmoving under the cover of darkness; the light only lifts the darkness and shows us what was sleeping beneath. And yet, it is not merely revelation, for as light falls on the land, not only do the day creatures (ourselves included) begin to wake and move in response to light's gentle touch, but the plants themselves begin to rise and stretch in the direction of the light. The light of morning not only reveals the landscape but also wakes up its inhabitants and orients life and movement toward itself.

There is a moment, though, when everything changes, when the gentle whisper of dawn becomes a sudden, apocalyptic shout. I use the word *apocalypse* in its original sense and meaning: an unveiling. A sunrise is an unveiling, the pulling back of a blanket of darkness, but in that final moment, it is not the landscape but the sun itself that is unveiled. Its golden edges spill like hot, melted gold over the horizon. It is beautiful and dangerous, illuminating and blinding. I want to look the sun in its face but rest my eyes instead on the transposed land. As he rises from his eastward bed, all that his fierce and blinding face rests upon is blessed, made both visible and beautiful.

Light is such an evasive thing, difficult to wrap our minds around since it seems always to be wrapping itself around our minds, the very thing by which we can perceive at all. Is it light I see on the newly christened morning or only its effects? Is it possible to see light or only see by it? It is difficult to describe light because it underpins our very ability to perceive; perhaps it is for its elusive but fundamental nature that the language of light has embedded itself in our language of the mind, of thought, of wisdom. Many of our ways of speaking of knowledge, wisdom, and understanding have bound up in them the imagery of light and dark, shadow and beam, night and sunrise.

## Standing under the Light

Take the word *enlighten*. To *enlighten* someone is to give them knowledge about a subject or situation, and usually *enlightening* information changes the whole manner in which we regard that person or idea or thing. "You think Christopher is such a nice person? Well, let me enlighten you . . ." Such a sentence is usually followed not only by a discrete fact, but by a new (and, in this case, perhaps darker) perspective. New knowledge or perspectives can *cast light* on a situation that we were previously *in the dark about*, the implication being that what we can know is in the light, and what we don't or can't know is in the dark.

How, then, do we come to know in this schema? Owen Barfield observes that "whatever word we hit on, if we trace its meaning far enough back, we find it apparently expressive of some tangible, or at all events, perceptible object or some physical activity. *Understanding* once meant 'standing under.'"[1] I imagine in my mind's eye the sunrise as its rays touch everything in my field of sight. *Standing-under* the sun, I gain an *under-standing* of the world in which I live; I am *enlightened*. What we usually mean by this word is not simply knowledge, or a vast collection of facts; we mean a vision of how all these things hang together. The difference between *enlightenment* and *knowledge* is like this: in the dark before dawn, I might know some facts about the landscape ahead of me—that there is a house somewhere, and an ocean—I might see a few things by the light of my phone flashlight, but when dawn comes, I witness them all together. Dawn does not give me a list of facts to remember, but a view of everything in its path.

We speak this way of people too. People can be *bright, brilliant* even, their ideas *lucid*, their books *illuminating*. A particularly erudite lecture can cause a *light bulb* to go off in our brains. The metaphor of understanding as light is so embedded in our language that we may often not even be aware of it.

Again, it seems that we use these metaphors of light to describe not what we see (the discrete topics of knowledge) but those perspectives by which we are able to see more clearly. What we mean is not just that these people or books say interesting or accurate things, but that they *shed light* on things in a way that is *clarifying* and *illuminating*, like the morning sun peeking over the edge of the horizon and making the outlines of the hills clear. In a fittingly apocalyptic passage, Daniel writes, "Those who are *wise* will shine as bright as the sky, and those who lead many to righteousness will shine like the stars forever" (12:3 NLT, italics added). Wise people become like the sun, and perhaps like the sun, we might even feel bashful about facing them; we feel a little blinded, happy only to see by the light of their brilliance.

In the Christian tradition and in Scripture, the most fundamental source of light and wisdom is God; God, the brilliant One by whom we can see all things. Jesus puts it most plainly in one of His "I Am" statements in the Gospel of John: "I am the light of the world. Whoever follows me will never walk in darkness, but will have the light of life" (8:12). The psalmist praises God again and again, singing, "The Lord is my light and my salvation" (Psalm 27:1) and boasts that "my God turns my darkness into light" (Psalm 18:28).

Those who find themselves in darkness, who do not know which way to go, need only turn to the One who is both Wisdom and Light. The apostle James puts it quite simply: "If any of you lacks wisdom, you should ask God, who gives generously to all without finding fault, and it will be given to you" (James 1:5). You might think that this has nothing to do with light, but near the end of the chapter, James refers again to this gift, and the God who gives good gifts: "Every generous act of giving, with every perfect gift, is from above, coming down from the Father of lights, with whom there is no variation or shadow due to change" (1:17 NRSVUE). God is light, without shifting shadows. God is wisdom, who gives generously. God is brilliant.

## The Light of Wisdom

Light and knowledge are practical necessities. Anyone who has tried to stumble their way to the bathroom in the dead of night without turning on a light will tell you this. We need light to know which way we are going, to feel secure and unafraid when our hand brushes an unexpectedly slimy substance on the kitchen counter, to avoid the sharp and dreadful pain of a stray Lego; in plain terms our capacity to *see* the Lego (because light has fallen on it) is close to our capacity to *know* where the Lego is and thus avoid it; but the same might be true of invisible things. We need *wisdom to light our path in life*; to know what sorts of relationships will destroy us, what things are worth pursuing. Without knowledge, we stumble through life stubbing our toes and grabbing at the wrong things.

The coupling of light with wisdom and darkness with ignorance pervades Scripture, particularly in the Wisdom literature. In the hopeful and nearly nihilistic pensée that is Ecclesiastes, the Quoheleth (teacher) writes, "I saw that wisdom excels folly as light excels darkness. The wise have eyes in their head, but fools walk in darkness" (2:13–14 NRSVUE). In these writings, wisdom as light acts as a guide on the way of life, a metaphor that could be explored in its own right. In a long celebration of God's laws revealed in the Torah, the psalmist proclaims, "I gain understanding from your precepts; therefore I hate every wrong path. Your word is a lamp for my feet, a light on my path" (Psalm 119:104–105).

The equation is quite simple when you think about it; in the light, we can see things, and thus gain *knowledge* about them; in the darkness, those things are hidden from us, and thus we are *ignorant* of them. To be in the dark, then, is to be in danger. We might fall, strike our foot on a rock, or be attacked by someone hiding in the dark. Wicked people hide in the dark, because no one can see what they're doing; no one will *know*. And it's not only hidden dangers that pervade the dark; it is lack of direction. We cannot *know* which path to take, or whether the path will have obstacles. In the dark, I do not *know* what to do, how to *orient* myself. The way is hidden from me. Without wisdom and understanding, the world is as dark as four in the morning, when anything might happen, any obstacle, foe, or slimy substance might find us, and we can't proceed with confidence.

In this sense, the relationship between understanding and action is like the way plants strain toward the sun, and the way that human activity begins to quicken beneath the rays of morning. We could imagine that all the sun does is reveal the landscape, that understanding and wisdom help us grasp the way things are. But the very process of revelation, of standing under the sun of gaining new knowledge, reorients us; we strain in the direction of wisdom like plants drawn to sunlight. Or, indeed, perhaps, on the contrary, we hide from knowledge, knowledge we know will require change or discomfort or confession. For one of the attributes of both the fool and the sinner is that they do their deeds in darkness. There are all kinds of reasons we might prefer to be ignorant, not to upset ourselves or the people in our house, so we keep the light off, and we step on the Lego.

Wisdom literature shows that avoiding the light has a ripple effect; when we hide from the light, we walk in darkness and become dark ourselves. Romans 1 speaks of those who ignore God's ways: "Their foolish hearts were darkened. Professing to be wise, they became fools" (vv. 21–22 NKJV).

The slippage between sin and ignorance is an interesting one too. To live rightly is not to follow a list of rules, but to live according to the way the world is; it's not to follow Google Maps' written instructions, but to be able to see the path ahead of you, enabling you to avoid stumbling over stones where they present themselves. People who cannot see their path (who are not living by the wisdom of God) might slip and fall, might hurt themselves. We could call this "sin" in the literal sense of "missing the mark," but not all fools are sinners. God is the one who gives wisdom, and God is the Light, in whom there are no shifting shadows. Peter writes, "We also have the prophetic message . . . and you will do well to pay attention to it, as to a light shining in a dark place, until the day dawns and the morning star rises in your hearts" (2 Peter 1:19). We live in a day of darkness and confusion, but Peter exhorts us not to be fools; pick up the lamp of the prophets and walk by its light. There is a difference between someone who has lived underground their whole life and someone who has seen the sunrise and chooses to live in a bunker.

## The True Inner Light

The entanglement of light and understanding applies not only to the practical truths of living but also to the pursuit of knowledge itself. How do we come to know something? What are the conditions of knowledge itself? These were questions Augustine of Hippo explored, picking up on that same theme of God as light and knowledge often in his description of the operations of the mind. Take, for instance, this passage about God as light:

> The earth is visible and light is visible but the earth cannot be seen unless it is brightened by light. So, likewise, for those which . . . everyone understands and acknowledges . . . to be most true, one must believe they cannot be understood unless they are illumined by something else as by their own sun. Therefore just as in the sun one may remark three certain things, namely that it is, that it shines, and that it illumines, so also in that most hidden God whom you wish to know there are three things, namely, that He is, that He is known, and that He makes other things to be known.[2]

The theme of God as the "light" and source of knowledge is so pervasive in Augustine that it has been given

69

the name illuminationism. Thousands upon thousands of pages have been written trying to decipher, defend, or deconstruct what exactly Augustine means by his close association between light and knowledge, whether he "has" a cognitive theory (a theory of how we think), and whether that light enables merely the capacity of thought or objects (or forms) of thought itself. In her rigorous book on that topic, Lydia Schumacher describes Augustine's dialogue with his son Adeodatus in *De Magistro* ("on the master") about the process of learning. Augustine and his son discuss together whether it is the teacher, or the words, or the students themselves that make it possible for genuine learning to occur, but summarizing their conclusion, Schumacher says Augustine claims that "divine illumination enacts the possibility of the teaching and learning, which would not otherwise be possible. He describes Christ as the inner Teacher, the light all consult to gain understanding."[3] Perhaps all this philosophizing is beyond me, but what I do see is Augustine circling around the mysterious ways in which God is involved in the very act of thinking.

Samuel Kimbriel writes that whatever else we may say about Augustine's cognitive theory (or lack thereof), Augustine conveys that "the Divine is always already present in the most intimate operations of the mind and that if this were not the case the human would cease to be what it is."[4] This means that very act of searching out the truth and trying to understand things is to stand under the Sun of God's illumination; it is knowing *by Him*. Kimbriel suggests that this is why Augustine so frequently opens even the most speculative of philosophical passages (with which we might not naturally connect a spiritual inclination) with a prayer, an invocation of the Light and Wisdom of God, because the act of seeking to know is always done in the light of God. Study is a spiritual matter; in seeking knowledge, we experience the warmth of God's light, which lightens us.

This could present to us an oddly passive idea of reason and knowledge; if we know through the illumination of God, what good is it to "try" to know anything? Mustn't we only wait to receive illumination? But here, too, the metaphor of light can guide us. You cannot make the sun shine, but you can go to a high place to watch the sunrise, or stand under the shadow of a tree, or hide in your house with all the curtains drawn. The metaphor of light as wisdom doesn't imply passivity in our search for enlightenment, but receptivity. Kimbriel suggests that the way Augustine returns to the theme of illuminationism is less like a proto-philosophy of the mind (as some scholars suggest), and more along the lines of a spiritual practice "whereby Augustine wrestles with his own infirmity so as to come to live within the logic of incarnation."[5] That light shines is a matter that has little to do with us. But to be able to see *by the light*, or, indeed, to *be enlightened*, there are various things we can do, practices we can adopt, and postures we can inhabit. These will either enable, prevent, or distract us from seeing the light. Here, I want to suggest that if we want to seek wisdom and its light, we can stand under the light, we can turn toward the light, we can wait for the light.

## Dissipate the Darkness Which Covers Us . . .

During my doctoral studies, I often attended a study group held at one of the student chaplaincies. Most of

71

postgraduate work is independent; you must set deadlines for yourself, keep yourself on track, and direct your own studies. It can be very lonely since you never *need* to see anyone other than your fellow sleep-deprived library rats, and very boundless since you must set your own schedule. The study group met three days a week. It began with morning prayer, followed by working sessions and breaks for coffee and lunch, and it ended with evening prayer. I appreciated the companionship and structure it offered, and its rhythms began to become my own. So, too, did its prayers. We began each day with the "Scholar's Prayer," usually attributed to that slow bull plodding after truth, Thomas Aquinas. It begins with this supplication: "Come, Holy Spirit, Divine Creator, true source of light and fountain of wisdom! Pour forth your brilliance upon my dense intellect, dissipate the darkness which covers me, that of sin and of ignorance."[6]

As I prayed this prayer each morning, working diligently away on the messy thesis draft that seemed like it would never be finished, I began to conceive of my own little efforts as a practice of *standing under the light*. There are a few things to note in this prayer. The first, of course, is that wisdom is set alongside, and almost indivisible from, light, and that God (more specifically the Holy Spirit) is the source of both light and wisdom. Once you begin to notice this metaphorical couple, you will see it everywhere. The second, which I find interesting, is the description of things that keep us *in the dark*: sin and ignorance. This resonates with the fool of Proverbs and the Psalms, who does not know where he is going, but here we are reminded that sin and ignorance might not only affect our moral lives and practical decisions but also the quality and clarity of our thoughts. Sin causes us to avoid the "source of light and fountain of wisdom," whereas ignorance merely represents someone who never has *seen the light*, or perhaps never been *shown the light*.

It reminds me of G. K. Chesterton's "madman" in *Orthodoxy*. He writes that we can become very convinced of a certain kind of narrow view of the world, and he prescribes this cure for the inadequate intellect: "If you or I were dealing with a mind that was growing morbid, we should be chiefly concerned not so much to give it arguments as to give it air, to convince it that there was something cleaner and cooler outside the suffocation of a single argument."[7]

Vices of fear, pride, and despair can keep us underground, counting the pebbles of our tiny bits of knowledge in the dark, but so can a simple lack of exposure to the world. If this all sounds very spiritual and abstract, you must think of it this way: we cannot describe the landscape if we are always inside because we are afraid of other people, or because we're too lazy. We must be able to see the world to know things about it. So sometimes seeking wisdom requires us to come out of the cave we have been hiding in due to sin. But what if it is ignorance that has prevented us from seeing the light? What if, in fact, we have never seen the light because no one has ever *shown us*, or even because we grew up in a world where knowledge, wisdom, and light were actively hidden? Where to begin?

*Turn toward the light.* We must also be able to ask for wisdom. Proverbs 4:7 gives the very tautological advice that "the beginning of wisdom is this: Get wisdom." In a TV show I love, in moments of fear and confusion, two characters will say to each other, "Tell me one true thing." This little island of truth, even if it is only as small a certainty as "I know I love the taste of this coffee" or "I know you have green eyes" becomes like a small stream of light in a dark place they can follow toward a deeper, more sustained truth. I think of this practice of turning toward the light as asking for wisdom. We do not usually ask for something with our backs to the person of whom we are requesting the thing. To turn toward wisdom is to turn our face in the direction of the light we find; it might at first be a very small piece of knowledge or light, but to ask for light is to turn toward it, to ask for more, and to follow its beam. I think this is why Aquinas begins his scholarly endeavors by *asking* God to illuminate him. To ask God for wisdom is to turn in the direction of light, to practice an openness to truth.

The final thing that considering light as wisdom might teach us is that sometimes the only way you can "get" wisdom (inasmuch as you can "get" light) is to *wait for the light*. The author of *Paradise Lost*, John Milton, plays with this idea of living in darkness in his famous poem Sonnet 19. He writes, "When I consider how my light is spent, Ere half my days, in this dark world and wide."[8] In his later years, Milton began to lose his sight, which prevented him from working as freely as he did in his younger years, and causing him to depend more on his daughter as an amanuensis. This loss of physical sight also led him to feel lost in life. Robbed of the ease with which he had pursued his calling of writing, he felt lost, unsure of how to proceed. He references this feeling of uselessness in the next line, bemoaning "that one Talent . . . Lodged with me useless."[9] Milton is like the psalmist or the prophet, lost in the dark, not it seems because of sin or of ignorance, but merely because of the nature of this "dark world"; sometimes the light is hidden to us not because of our own ignorance or sin, or because God is hiding, but because it is a confusing, broken, and difficult world.

Milton's poem has returned to me and been meaningful to me at many different periods in my life. I have felt its pain when I did not know which path to take in life and wondered what I should do next. I have chewed on its words when I did know what I wanted to do, when I felt ready to give myself to and serve someone, something, or some place, when I knew, even what I wanted to do, but that vocation felt stifled, obstructed, impossible. I have felt it perhaps most keenly when I sought to *know*, to understand and believe in God, but God seemed to hide from me, to not care about my earnest search for Him, to not give an answer to my honest questions. In those seasons, I want to say I've done everything I can to find wisdom, to turn toward it, to ask for it, but part of me knows I am also limited and flawed, or perhaps I failed in some way.

And then, many of us may experience the epistemological uncertainty of having been brought up in an environment that lied to us or obscured the truth; how can we begin to know what is true when we cannot know who to trust, when our very capacity to know and to trust has been bruised? Perhaps this is what the prophet Micah felt when he wrote "The faithful have been swept from the land; not one upright person remains," (7:2) cautioning his reader, "Do not trust a neighbor; put no confidence in a friend" (v. 5). The world where he lives is all threat, all darkness. He does not know where he can go because he does not know what or whom he can trust, what knowledge is reliable, what is truth and what is a lie.

The conclusion of Micah's thoroughly pessimistic account of the world in which he finds himself is this: "I watch in hope for the Lord, I wait for God my Savior . . . though I sit in darkness, the Lord will be my light" (vv. 7–8). There is something beautiful in this; even as he feels betrayed by every source of both authority and friendship, even when he does not know which way to look, he waits. And in his waiting, it seems there is a hope. In his waiting, he has already started to turn to the light, like the plants that begin to turn their faces toward the sun that hasn't risen yet. They wait in hope.

## Waiting for Wisdom

And this is where Milton arrives, patiently awaiting the sun to rise over the deep darkness of early morning. As far as he can tell, he has done all he can to navigate "this dark world and wide" and, indeed, his soul is "more bent to serve . . . My Maker" than ever. Sometimes we find ourselves in the dark not because of sin or ignorance but merely because it is a broken world. There is nothing you can do to make the sun rise, and no shame in needing a flashlight because the clouds have covered the moon. Indeed, when you find yourself waiting for the light, know that this vigil is a holy one, because, as Milton concludes his sonnet: "They also serve who only stand and wait."[10]

#  LIVING, THINKING, PRAYING

This is the message we have heard from him and declare to you: God is light; in him there is no darkness at all. If we claim to have fellowship with him and yet walk in the darkness, we lie and do not live out the truth. But if we walk in the light, as he is in the light, we have fellowship with one another, and the blood of Jesus, his Son, purifies us from all sin.

1 John 1:5–7

## ■ LIVING METAPHORS

Find time to watch a sunrise, whether it is with another person or on your own. Give your full attention to the rising sun, except perhaps to take a picture of the dark horizon or to write down a description of it. Pick an object, a vista, or a spot on the horizon to check in on as the sunrise progresses; what does the light do to the object of your attention? What does it reveal? Highlight?

## ■ THINKING AND PRAYING

*Prayer*: "Canticle" in Morning Prayer, in North Umbrian Daily Office

*Poem*: "Pangur Ban," ninth-century Old Irish Poem. Recommended translation: Seamus Heaney

*Film*: *The Secret of Kells*

*Architecture*: The Guggenheim Museum

*Art*: "Blind Light," Antony Gormley (2007)

*Music*: "The Light," Regina Spektor

These works of art are concerned with light and with wisdom. The Celtic canticle invokes Christ's enlightening presence at the beginning of each day, to illumine the path before the person who prays.[11]

Seamus Heaney's translation of the remarkable ninth-century poem "Pangur Ban" opens a window into the life of a Celtic scribe hard at work on a manuscript. The scribe of this poem would have been responsible for transcribing the manuscripts of the Gospels and other ancient texts, a task necessary to the study and life of worship that sustained the Celtic church in the tumultuous era of warfare and destruction that characterized those years of Viking raids. Kept company by a cat seeking mice with diligent attention, the scribe describes his task of transcribing manuscripts as "turning darkness into light," imagining the pursuit of knowledge as an almost magical vocation. The animated film *The Secret of Kells* visualizes this vocation, adding a further theme of the fear that can close us off to the outside world; when fear rules, it darkens our hearts and perspective.

The architecture of the Guggenheim Museum plays with the use of light in space. Often when we think about light, we imagine it landing on a flat plane, where we are either illumined or not illumined. But the Guggenheim shows how illumination happens within a spatial context, where we might move toward or away from light; light orients us and draws us onward. In contrast to this, Antony Gormley's piece explores the way in which light can obscure and blind. It is comprised of a glass-paneled room into which people can enter, fitted out with bright lights and humidifiers. Gormley writes, "You enter this interior space that is the equivalent of being on top of a mountain or at the bottom of the sea."[12] And yet this interior space is too bright to see anything; it is disorienting. This can cause us to think about the nature of knowledge. Can we become blinded by knowledge? Why does this happen? What role does context play in our capacity to know and be oriented? What does it say about wisdom and light if we can only bear a little bit at a time?

Regina Spektor's intimate little song recounts the in-between state of wakefulness, when she feels vulnerable and open and a little afraid, the morning light having woken her.[13] She thinks about her life and recounts the things she "knows" but is left with a sense of anxiety for those she loves, having fretted the night before. Three times she reminds herself that "the morning is wiser than the evening," to not dwell on the fears of the shadowy nighttime. In the morning she is more able to receive the mysteries of her life as a gift, asked only to open up her eyes.

# SAFETY
## IS (NOT)
# A FORTRESS

He lifted me out of the slimy pit, out of the mud
    and mire;
he set my feet on a rock and gave me a firm place
    to stand.

Psalm 40:2

Castle walls just lead me to despair.
Don McLean, "Castles in the Air"

**L**et me make a confession: I hate the London Underground. I work in London now, and amongst my expat friends in London there is an attitude of sentimental affection surrounding the Tube. When we board, quietly judging all the tourists, popping in our AirPods or pulling out our books, we can pretend we are *true* Londoners. My friends find it thrilling in a quotidian way, charming in a grimy way.

I do not share this sentiment. I descend the stairs into Charing Cross as if descending into hell. A warm air from some obscure source blows hair into my mouth, making me feel warm and sticky, as if someone is breathing in my ear. Where does the air come from? Why is it warm? Better not to dwell on these questions. A group of tourists is blocking the gates, innocently causing anguish and resentment in commuters like me with somewhere to be. I overtake the tourists, but not quickly enough. Someone's backpack bumps me, and as I am recovering from the offense someone else cuts me off in the line to scan my travel card. The impossibly long escalator is broken; the escalator stairs are slightly too tall, thus the crowd descends haltingly into the belly of the beast.

Finally, we board the train. Now I am in an oversized tin can with several dozen strangers, some of whom are unaccountably yelling and laughing very loudly. The train shudders to a start, the tracks screeching as we pick up speed. The basic engineering of the train has not changed significantly since the 1800s, a fact which is announced to me through the violent shaking unique, in my experience, to the Bakerloo line. If you stay on long enough, the lights will go out at least twice. No one seems to notice. I close my eyes. This will be over soon. But then, the train stops, and not at a platform. I could not tell you where we are, only that it is utterly dark outside, that I am stuck, and I can feel the closeness of the walls. *Perhaps this is it*, I say to myself, reconciled to this cramped end.

"My apologies, ladies and gentlemen," a bored voice announces over crackling speakers. "We are held up by a train at the next stop. We'll be on our way shortly." *But what if we aren't on our way shortly?* I think. What if I die in this stuffy, suffocating tin can of strangers? Or worse yet, what if I have to sit here in the dirt and noise and dark for thirty minutes? I take a deep breath through my nose to calm down, a tactic which is hardly useful given the air quality down here. And then, a jolt. Movement. Relief. We're on our way again. Two more stops and we arrive at Paddington. I hasten into the cool air of the spacious station. A deep breath, a sigh of relief. I have survived once again.

*Anxiety.* That is what I feel as I descend the stairs into the caverns of the London Underground. *Relief.* That is what I feel when the fresh air fills my lungs on the street. Don't get me wrong: I heartily support a good public transportation system and am grateful for the ability to get from point A to point B in a relatively efficient manner. But I find the whole ordeal of being underground with strangers in a fast-moving metal tube distressing.

Granted, you could probably say that I have a higher level of anxiety when it comes to underground trains than the average person, but much of what makes the Tube anxiety-inducing for me involves phobias that are not uncommon in the general population: small spaces, crowds, the dark, being buried alive. I am not alone in this constellation of fears. We have this pull, it seems, as human beings, to ascend, to move upward, where we can see and breathe more clearly; it feels safer, less threatening, more full of possibilities.

This desire to *ascend* and *rise*, and the fear of falling *down*, or being caught *under*, is reflected in our ways of speaking about safety, security, and success. Often, to be *down* or *under* is to be disadvantaged or even in danger, whereas to be *up*, or rather, *on top*, is to be both safe and successful. Think of how we use the word *under*. I am *under attack*; she is *under the control* of that wicked man; their organization is *under scrutiny*; he was *under the influence of alcohol*. To be under is to be controlled or besieged. We might use *under* to describe a positive force of control over us (like being *under freedom*) but to do so is to play on the irony of the inherent dominative nature of the word.

When someone seeks to hurt or control us with their words, they *put us down* or *take us down a notch*. We speak, too, of failure in terms of *decline, inferiority, downfall*, weaknesses one cannot *rise above*. One can be *down and out*, at the *bottom of the pack*, an *underdog, kicked while they're down, dogpiled, buried, depressed*. All these words have a metaphoric gravitational pull downward. Danger is *down there*; safety and success are *up there*.

No wonder I fear the Tube.

In both thought and habit, we associate being high up with being safe and secure, and being down low with being vulnerable. In their book *Metaphors We Live By*, cognitive linguists George Lakoff and Mark Johnson note the prevalence of "orientational metaphors" like this, observing that "these spacial orientations arise from the fact that we have bodies of the sort we have and that they function as they do in our physical environment" and that our "metaphorical orientations are not arbitrary. They have a basis in our physical and cultural experiences."[1] Saint Augustine illustrated this point rather well in his sermon on the tenth chapter of John's Gospel:

> So also in our own body, the head is above, the feet are on the earth; yet in any crowding and throng of men, when any one treads on your foot, does not the head say, "You are treading upon me?" No one has trodden on your head, or on your tongue; it is above, in safety, no harm has happened unto it; and yet because by the bond of charity there is unity from the head even to the feet, the tongue does not separate itself therefrom, but says, "You are treading upon me;" when no one has touched it.[2]

Though he is making the point for his own other purposes, the message is clear: toes are disadvantaged because they are "down there" and easily trodden on; heads are safe because they are "up here" and harder to strike.

We associate *down* with danger and failure, falling and being hurt, drooping with weariness, being stuck underneath something or someone, being buried. In contrast to this, our associations with *up* as safe and promising are tied with experiences like reaching the top of a hill after a long hike, or even the experience of coming up for air after swimming deep in a swimming pool, the relief and triumph of that first breath. I want to consider how unearthing our innate assumptions about these various states might help us reckon with that powerful fear of falling and being caught under, and might help us stand up again.

## Safety Is (Not) a Castle

The city of Edinburgh sits on top of a hill overlooking the vast inlet and the mighty bridges that connect it with the northern part of the country. The city itself is a winding labyrinth of little alleyways and back passages, many of which are lined with stairs, because everything is on an incline. Everything is up, up, up, or down, down, down, and those who count flights of stairs and steps on their phone will be exhilarated and exhausted by the end of a day's exploration. If you climb your way up Victoria Street and the Royal Mile, you'll find yourself in front of the gates to the old castle. This site has been a fortress for over a millennium, though it has changed hands many times, often through siege. Though it was inhabited long before, its oldest remnant is the chapel built in honor of Queen Margaret of Scotland by her son in the early twelfth century. It was an important point of defense during turbulent times of marauding enemies and struggles for power; whoever took the castle held, quite literally, the *high ground*. So highly valued was this castle that it is thought to be one of the most besieged castles in all of the United Kingdom. When it comes to warfare, the castle's location gave it three advantages: a good view, reaction time, and a good posture of defense.

From the "Castle Rock," as it was known in more ancient times, you can see many, many miles in any direction. This would give a keen-eyed watchman not only a few hours, but possibly a few days of warning. The view itself offered the gift of time—time to react, time to defend, time to prepare. The heightened position was also an advantage for attack. Defensive strategies depended on the height of the castle; one strategy that stuck with me was pouring boiling oil on the enemy as they attempted to scale the wall; they not only fought their enemies, they fried them.

During the War for Scottish Independence, to be on low ground was to be less prepared for attack. And, indeed, the Lowlands were notoriously violent, insecure places. When you cannot see clearly or very far in any direction, you are at a greater risk of attack, and at greater risk of an attack to which you might not have time to respond. The lower you are, the easier it is for enemies to reach and to strike you; to *kick someone while they are down* is not only cruel but easier. It struck me that the reputation of violence in the Lowlands might be connected to its geographic positioning. If you are constantly under threat, if you never feel safe, you will always be ready to fight. One might become violent out of habitual need. I wonder if this is the case with combative and defensive people; perhaps they feel like they live in the Lowlands, never safe.

The Bible often uses strongholds and castles as metaphors for safety and security. Much of the Bible itself was written in a time of tumult similar to that of medieval Scotland. Indeed, much of the narrative arc of the Hebrew Bible has to do with the capture, captivity, and release of various kingdoms, so considerations of war, security, defense, and attack would have been comprehensible and relevant to its contemporary readers. And yet, while these metaphors draw on the lived experience of a society where warfare was not uncommon, the writers of wisdom literature often apply these metaphors to the emotional and spiritual experiences of insecurity and threat, whether that threat derives from violence, loss of friends, loss of money, or loss of confidence.

Proverbs 18:10 declares, "The name of the Lord is a fortified tower; the righteous run to it and are safe." A tower: height, protection, security. This is immediately contrasted with another source of security and protection: wealth. "The wealth of the rich is their fortified city; they imagine it a wall too high to scale" (18:11). It's interesting how similar these two verses are, though there are some small but important differences. In the first verse the group seeking safety is the righteous, and in the second it is the rich. Both have a metaphorical "strong tower" or "fortified city" to which they turn in trouble; and it is worth noting that the wealthy think wealth is not only a fortified tower but also a fortified city. The verse implies that the wealthy imagine wealth to be a step above a plebeian tower. Money can't buy happiness, but it can buy moats. Trusting the tower of God is for poor folk who can't afford drawbridges. The final difference is the perceived and actual safety of their chosen refuge: the rich "imagine" their wealth to be "too high to scale" while "the righteous run to" their tower and "are safe." The implication is that the tower of the Lord is safer than the city of the wealthy.

Most of us are not wealthy and may laugh at the idea of regarding wealth as a city of refuge, but there are other towers to which we might turn when we are threatened. Social connections, for instance, or talent. In a passage of the devastating *Neapolitan Quartet* by pseudonymous Elena Ferrante, one of the characters who has grown up in a chaotic environment of poverty and abuse reflects on the refuge that her fiancé's financially stable family will offer: "I was about to enter a protective family, a sort of well-fortified castle from which I could proceed without fear or to which I could retreat if I were in danger."[3]

This passage puts the search for security quite clearly, but it is a theme that permeates the whole series, which is soaked through with fear and insecurity. The book follows the lives of two young women, Lena and Lila, growing up in post-war Naples, Italy, and is riddled with violence, poverty, and corruption. Through this maelstrom, Lena and Lila seek means not only of security but also of agency. Ways to both make themselves safe and make themselves known. Lena, the narrator, holds on to her intellect as a means of security, her ticket to the party of life, before trying her hand at social connections, at romance, even at money, and perhaps most fundamentally, friendship. In all these means of stability, Lena and Lila find unstable castles, dissolving margins, which leave them terrified. Their actions are often cruel because they are afraid.

Most of our experiences of insecurity and fear will not be as extreme as those of Lila and Lena, but we too will be afraid, and we too will seek our castles and our strongholds from which to proceed: work, friendship, money, romance, social connections. I think it is important to acknowledge these things do offer stability. Proverbs does not directly say that wealth is not a source of security—its pages are full of wisdom about working, saving, lending, and not extorting others. The wealthy imagine that wall cannot be scaled because, perhaps, it is a wall that does offer some security. But there is a fragility, a contingency about the stability of these things; friends can die and be fickle, money can be lost in the downturn of a market. If we are to be truly safe, it must not be a safety that is never touched by the fragility and violence of the world, but a safety that can endure it.

I love the way Julian of Norwich writes about this in *Revelations of Divine Love*. Julian, if that truly was her name, was born in 1342 to a hazardous world. Her lifetime was overshadowed by the plague, which came in recurrent waves to her home city of Norwich. The Peasants Revolt of 1381 saw violence, public executions, and economic devastation engulf the city. Julian herself received the visions that comprise her book during a near-death experience. She was no stranger to fear, to danger, to illness. And yet safety is one of the themes around which she circles again and again. In one of her visions she writes, "If any such lover be in earth which is continually kept from falling, I know it not: for it was not shewed me. But this was shewed: that in falling and in rising we are ever preciously kept in one Love."[4]

Julian became an Anchorite, a monastic role that involved confining oneself to a cell in or underneath a church, praying, and making oneself available to the spiritual needs of the townspeople. For the second half of her life she was quite literally ensconced, not in a castle, high and inaccessible, but in a cave, available to all who sought her counsel. The safety she describes is an existential safety, one that cannot be touched by fear, violence, or even death. It is the miraculous safety that Beyoncé describes at the conclusion of *Lemonade*, when after reckoning with the unfaithfulness of her husband, she finds that the marriage has been not only preserved but also reborn: "My grandma said, 'Nothing real can be threatened.'"[5]

Dwelling on the metaphor of castles that do (and do not) offer safety gives me a new way to engage with those all-encompassing and sticky feelings of fear and insecurity. When I feel afraid and vulnerable, ready to strike out in cruel fear or curl up in a ball and avoid all action in the world, I have started to ask myself: how might I steal away to a place of perspective and of shelter? How can I give myself the buffer of reaction time? Perhaps I should not contemplate pouring boiling oil on the heads of my enemies or problems, but these allies—time, perspective, and shelter—can make us feel safe enough not to react in the red-hot flash of anger or the frozen compliance of fear. And even when I cannot find this safety in myself, how can I run to the fortified tower of the God who loves me, and in whose love I am kept, as Dame Julian puts it, very safe?

## Climbing the Ladder of Success

There are many ways to fail in this life. Let me name a few. One way you might fail is by not *living up* to your potential. When you were little, parents and caregivers looked at you with a special twinkle in their eye. "This one will do well," they seemed to say (and sometimes actually said). You liked the attention and the affirmation, and you endeavored to deserve them. But somewhere along the way you *tripped up*, you failed a test or married a deadbeat, or perhaps, through no fault of your own, the doors of opportunity simply shut, and try as you might, you would only ever be normal. People don't like to admit it, but you *let them down*. You *fell short* of what you might have been; you're a *letdown*.

You might also fail by simply never having potential to begin with. Perhaps you were *born at the bottom of the pack*—life was stacked against you. You're not, in the proper sense, a failure, because there were no *heights of expectation* from which you could fall. You failed merely by not being able to *climb out* of poverty or mediocrity. Perhaps worst of all, you have failed by first succeeding and then failing utterly. Unlike your disappointing colleagues who never lived up to their potential, you had *upward mobility*. Your goals were *lofty*, your tactics efficient. You know what it meant to be *on top of your game*. You *climbed the ladder* of success, graciously refusing to step on the fingers of the opponents you *surpassed*. You have reached great heights, and then by some fault or accident, you *tumbled off the pedestal* everyone built for you, or you for yourself. Your presiding feeling is one of embarrassment, shame. You don't like to hear them whisper, *Oh, how the mighty have fallen.*

One way of thinking about these metaphors is to think of *success as a ladder we must climb*. The higher we climb, the safer and more impressive we are; the lower we are, the more vulnerable and disappointing we are. It's okay to be on the bottom for a while, but only if you climb, climb, climb. The image of a ladder is clearly hierarchical: there are definite points of higher and lower progress; there are measured points of success, goals that if you do not reach you will have failed. This metaphor is competitive in a zero-sum way; it's hard for two people to be at the same point on a ladder, and the process of passing someone on a ladder would involve some force, awkwardness, and the distinct possibility of knocking someone off of the ladder. It also entails a certain inevitability; once you've climbed to a certain point on the ladder, you cannot easily get off the ladder. Indeed, it's an odd inversion of the castle metaphor; once you are high up enough on the ladder, you become endangered, fearful you might fall (or be pushed) off. The only way to stay safe is to keep climbing.

As women began to enter the workforce, a metaphor evolved to describe this dynamic: *the glass ceiling.* This metaphor describes the experiences of women who cannot seem to get past a certain point in the hierarchy of a profession or in success. We can see an advancement but are stopped by the invisible glass ceiling that seems impossible to break. *The glass ceiling* is a matter of safety, not for women, but for men; it "protects" a certain kind of man from having to deal with or compete against competent women. Women seem to have to fight for a corner of a rung to hang on to, helping each other stay on the ladder even when they're not sure if it's safe.

The *glass ceiling* reveals the dangerous nature of the *ladder as success metaphor*: it has to do with status, and it is a zero-sum understanding of success. It assumes there is one point of safety (success), that the way to get there is alone, and that we all start at *the same point on the ladder*. If we are not reaching higher, we assume it is because we have not tried hard enough. We believe that being *higher on the ladder is better*, safer; higher on the ladder there is less clamoring, less chance of getting stuck. The ladder invites us to see each other as competitors: your triumph is my defeat. This mindset pervades our world, where politicians and businesspeople divide themselves into winners and losers. This metaphor has had profoundly negative effects on our society, making every realm of public life— politics, academia, economy—into a competitive warfare for resources and status. I do not want to suggest that competition in itself is bad. There is something glorious, pleasing, and fitting about pushing ourselves to master a skill or profession, to become better, to advance, to be a leader in a field. These are not evil aspirations, and indeed can be for the great good of many people. But is there a way to conceive of competition that is not zero sum? That is not violence?

Perhaps the metaphor of *climbing* need not be abandoned but expanded; perhaps we should consider climbing a mountain rather than a ladder. On a mountain there is still a sense of ascent, of goals achieved, of mastery and triumph. But on a mountain, there is space for many people to ascend at the same time, space to watch and learn from how another person ascends, room to bend and help someone else who has fallen down. There are also many ways up a mountain; success need not look the same for every person, need not happen at the same pace, need not take the same route. It is more difficult for one group of people to block a whole other group of people from ascending a mountain than a ladder. And when it comes to a mountain, the top is not always the best place to be; it is bright, unshielded, exposed to the elements. Replacing the ladder with the mountain keeps us from unnecessarily idolizing the top and gives us an image of ascent and mastery that is closer to *flourishing* than *success*. Shouldn't we judge our lives not by the binary of success and failure, but more by the context of our flourishing? Climb if you can, and climb if you must, but remember: the top of a ladder is lonely, but we can stand together on a mountain.

## Hell Is (Not) in the Basement

Perhaps the most potent reasons we associate being *dragged down* with threat is because of its strong connotations with death. We joke that an adversary won't rest until we are *six feet under*. This metaphor is very close to not being a metaphor; it is very nearly simply a fact. When we die, we are usually buried, rendered permanently *below, beneath, under* the realm of ordinary human existence. In the Hebrew Bible, going "*down* to Sheol" is one of the principal phrases used to describe death. In Genesis 37, Jacob refuses to be comforted after thinking his beloved child Joseph has been killed: "Surely I will *go down* to Sheol in mourning for my son" (v. 35 NASB, italics added). Job speaks ominously of Sheol, saying, "When a cloud vanishes, it is gone; in the same way one who *goes down* to Sheol does not come up" (7:9 NASB, italics added). A recurrent cry of the psalmist is that God save him from going down to Sheol, reasoning with God that it will be no good for God to save him when

YOU ARE A TREE

he's already *gone down* to Sheol: "Shall Your lovingkindness be declared in the grave? . . . Shall Your wonders be known in the dark? And Your righteousness in the land of forgetfulness?" (Psalm 88:11–12 NKJV). So here, too, *down* is associated not only with danger but also with demise, the ultimate demise of death.

Sometimes this fear of the *underworld* is a fear not only of *death* but also of hell and punishment. We speak furtively of *down there* as the place where wicked people go (though surely, hopefully, not us). Sheol was not understood in exactly the same way as we might think of hell; it was a place of stillness and darkness to which one descends upon death, where the souls of the dead go when the body has died, seemingly whether one was righteous or sinful. It bore similarities to the ancient Greek myths about Hades, the place of the dead ruled by its founder (and the source of its name), Hades.

The *Divine Comedy* has shaped our imagination of hell perhaps more than Scripture or myth. Its fourteenth-century author, Dante Alighieri, literally portrays hell as *beneath us*, deep in the fiery crust of the earth. The main character is led deeper and deeper into hell, farther and farther beneath the earth, and farther also into the torments sin exacts on its own transgressors. Only when Virgil and Dante come to purgatory do they begin a gradual upward journey that will ultimately lead to empyrean, the home of the blessed, paradise, a realm of light beyond time and space. In Dante's imagination the distinction could not be clearer: *upward* is blessedness, eternal life, union with God; *downward* is sin, damnation, frustration, dissatisfaction.

"He descended into the underworld" (*descendit ad inferos*). When many of us read these words, the vision that comes to mind might be something like a superhero or a Greek myth. In fact, this is a line from the Apostles' Creed, which many Christians recite each week in their Sunday worship. It references something that is known as *Anastasis* or the Harrowing of Hell, a medieval notion of what Jesus did in between dying and rising again; namely, freeing all the righteous dead from the dominion of death. This idea is often attributed to 1 Peter 4:6, which declares that "the gospel was preached even to those who are dead" (ESV) as well as Ephesians 4:9, which says that Christ "descended into the lower parts of the earth" (NKJV). Descended. Downward. To the dead, who are literally and figuratively *under the earth*.

This conjecture about what Jesus got up to between the cross and resurrection was a favorite subject of medieval art, and many stained-glass windows are devoted to the dramatic scene. My favorite depiction is by the Italian Dominican friar and painter Fra Angelo. In his rendition, a freshly risen Jesus, with wounds still in His feet from the crucifixion and a flag of victory waving behind a metallic halo, reaches out his right hand to Adam, pulling him and all who have died out of the cavern of death and into the light of eternal life. A crowd of people (Eve, John the Baptist, and all the righteous dead who have come before) is rushing out of a dark twisting hallway, like Londoners out of the Tube at peak hour. Crushed almost cartoonishly *under* (and it is worth noting the significance of this *inferior* position) the door to hell is the devil, his horns just peaking over the top of the door; the devil is incapacitated, looking almost silly, his cronies running to a tiny corner in fear.

Whatever you may make of the *Anastasis* and its artistic inheritance, its vivid imagery brings back to the central stage a core tenet of Christianity: Jesus rescues us from death, by death. He willingly *descends to the dead* to rescue them. He does not merely zap them out but goes where they are and rescues them. Death is inconceivable, but I find comfort in images of the resurrection. They remind me that there are no depths to which I can descend where God will not be with me, that Christ has not already plunged to rescue me. The psalmist writes, "If I ascend to heaven, you are there! If I make my bed in Sheol, you are there" (139:8 ESV). No matter how far I descend, even to death, I am not alone. Christ is with me. And He very well may crush the devil under the doors of death just like a Looney Tunes villain.

## Riding the High

The Tube isn't all bad. There's also the London overground. This train runs not in the secret tunnels, but on a high rail through the ins and outs of the city. You float like a pigeon over Canary Wharf with all its empty grandeur and flashy gestures to financial promise, you pass by the London Eye with its expensive sightseeing pods, and you cross the Thames in all its murky glory. To ride it at sunset or sunrise is the best—as the city, its charming and its run-down bits, is cast in the complimentary light of evening or dawn, golden and forgiving. When I ride the overground, I feel like I'm on *top of the world*, and everyone is there with me. And I must confess: I do love it.

# LIVING, THINKING, PRAYING

And Mary said:
"My soul glorifies the Lord
    and my spirit rejoices in God my Savior,
for he has been mindful
    of the humble state of his servant.
From now on all generations will call me blessed,
    for the Mighty One has done great things for me—
    holy is his name.
His mercy extends to those who fear him,
    from generation to generation.
He has performed mighty deeds with his arm;
    he has scattered those who are proud in their
        inmost thoughts.
He has brought down rulers from their thrones
    but has lifted up the humble.
He has filled the hungry with good things
    but has sent the rich away empty.
He has helped his servant Israel,
    remembering to be merciful
to Abraham and his descendants forever,
    just as he promised our ancestors."

Luke 1:46–55

## LIVING METAPHORS

Think of an experience in your everyday life where you descend somewhere without windows. Perhaps it is to your basement, to retrieve a suitcase in storage, or an underground public transportation system. How do you feel as you descend—do you get nervous, and, if so, what makes you nervous? The dark? The feeling of being underneath and the fear of getting stuck? How does it feel when you emerge from "down there" (wherever down is)?

Try to connect this thought experiment in your mind to your emotional experiences of security and insecurity. Think of when you feel the most confident, the most secure. What are you doing—are you displaying a competence for which you can garner praise and earn money, or are you next to someone you love, someone whose strengths lift you up, help you rise to the task of life?

Now think of something that makes you feel afraid. Where can you go—physically, emotionally, relationally—to obtain distance, perspective, and time? What tower of safety can you climb into?

## ■ THINKING AND PRAYING

*Hymn:* "Ein feste Burg ist unser Gott" ("A Mighty Fortress Is Our God"), Martin Luther

*Image: Fortress of Königstein from the North* (1756), Bernardo Bellotto

*Song:* "The Mountain," Jon Foreman

*Film: Knives Out* (2019), Rian Johnson

These words and works of art explore the theme of height as security and safety. The hymn, written by Protestant Reformer Martin Luther between 1527 and 1529, is one of the most beloved and familiar in Christian hymnody. Its opening lines draw on Psalm 46 and speak of God as a source of safety and love in a chaotic and treacherous world full of demonic opposition and earthly powers that would tempt and seek to destroy the Christian.

Bellotto's landscape portrait of the *Fortress of Königstein from the North* (1756) provides a vivid picture of the kind of security Luther pictures in the "feste Burg" (mighty fortress); raiding the stronghold of Königstein would involve an exhausting trek up a tall hill, only to be met by impenetrable walls of stone. No wonder the mighty Konig (King) felt safe; only God, it seems, could cast down a throne nestled in the likes of these walls.

Of course, reaching a place of safety, climbing toward a place where we can see ourselves and the world around us can itself be a frightening experience. Jon Foreman meditates on this in his song "The Mountain," resolving to ascend the mountain and not give in to the fear that causes him to hide.

But as Luther's hymn reminds us, earthly power is no match to the power of God. In Mary's magnificent song, known throughout history as the *magnificat* for its opening lines in Latin, she praises God for His mighty deeds and faithfulness. The theme of her song is the *elevation of the humble* and the *humbling of the high-minded*: God has "brought down rulers from their thrones" and "lifted up the humble" (v. 52). The image of a mighty and elevated throne being thrown down and a kneeling peasant being elevated is gripping and apocalyptic, especially in the imperial world in which Mary lived.

The 2019 murder mystery film *Knives Out* seems to play with this scriptural imagery. Fran, the protagonist and housekeeper of the self-made novelist, is portrayed as a Marian figure, lifted up in her humility over the entitled and wealthy family. So pure of heart that she vomits every time she attempts to lie, Fran is associated visually with Mary in the final scenes through a halo of knives pointed down at her, an homage to the popular depiction of Mary as Our Lady of Sorrows. The film explores sources of security dubious and deep, status, money, and power, as well as truth telling, trust, and human relationships. The movie begins and ends on a balcony overlooking the driveway of the wealthy mystery writer's house, concluding with Fran overlooking the crowd, a vivid depiction of the proud brought down from their thrones and the humble lifted up.

# LOVE
## IS (NOT)
# A DISEASE

Jesus replied, "Anyone who loves me will obey my teaching. My Father will love them, and we will come to them and make our home with them."

John 14:23

Love is not love
Which alters when it alteration finds,
Or bends with the remover to remove.
O no! it is an ever-fixed mark
That looks on tempests and is never shaken.

William Shakespeare, Sonnet 116

What does love look like to you? What does it feel like? To me, it looks like the soft, black lashes of the person I love, staring in concentration at a book. It smells like a meal prepared for me after a long-awaited homecoming, like pipe smoke, like laundry detergent, like a new baby's peach-fuzz head. Love sounds like laughter, my own name called out to me with playful correction or the tenderness of deep knowledge. Love feels like warmth, comfort, ease, arms in which I can totally relax. It tastes like a cup of tea I didn't make, like lips that have made and kept promises to me.

The experience of love is, for most of us, visceral. And this is the case not only in its abundant presence but also in its tragic absence. We feel the abandonment of love, the betrayal of love in our stomachs, between our eyes, welling up in our throats, or making our whole bodies numb. Love and its wreckages form much of the poetry and meaning of human existence. When we love someone, we feel this rhapsodic necessity to describe what is precious about them, and what is amusing, confusing, compelling.

When we lose love, be it through abandonment, death, or betrayal, we feel sick until we know how to speak the loss of it out loud. It feels important to be able to speak about love, even as it feels impossible to do so. When we love someone, whether it is a lover or a child or even sometimes a very,

very dear friend, they *become our world,* and so we use our whole world to describe them, because everything reminds us of the beloved. This is particularly poignant in grief, when the whole world becomes a reminder of the beloved, everything in its presence a reminder of absence; they are everywhere and nowhere we look. And what we want to describe is not only the beloved but also the love itself, this force that overcomes us and orients us in the world.

Love is so integral to our lives that we seem to use almost everything to describe it. And each of those descriptions shapes how we think about love—whether it is dangerous, nourishing, or even possible. And with each of the metaphors we place ourselves in different postures toward love, different points of access, different levels of safety. Though there are innumerable metaphors for the mysterious and undoing experience of love, I propose to look at three that, I think, relate to each other in various ways: love as a sickness, love as a home, love as a mirror.

## Love Is (Not) an Unfortunate Situation

Many of the ways we describe love are violent or distressing. We *fall* in love, like it's a pool we've slipped into, after committing the cardinal sin of lifeguards: running too quickly on the slippery cement of infatuation. Love can *drive us mad.* When we say someone is *crazy about his girlfriend,* we usually mean it kindly, happily; we mean he loves her *to distraction.* Sometimes love can even make us sick, *lovesick* that is, like it's a bad flu you can catch on the train from a stranger when you least expect it. These metaphors betray our fear and perhaps our experience of love as hazardous, something that takes us over and disturbs our normal ways of being and thinking, a power over which we have very little control.

These idioms describing love as a sickness, a madness, and a hazard are as old as the hills, or at least as old as ancient Athens, where they're explored in one of ancient philosophy's most treasured texts: *The Phaedrus*. In it, Plato describes a discourse between Socrates and the young, bright orator Phaedrus. It's a strange text, often much stranger than the contexts in which I have encountered it have allowed themselves to admit. It is an intermingling of philosophy, rhetoric, and seduction, where one can never tell exactly which one is being discussed or practiced. Socrates and Phaedrus attempt to bewitch and seduce each other as they take turns with their speeches crafted to evoke the emotions they describe: desire, lust, and perhaps most of all, *lovesickness*. Their theatrical conversation circles around many topics, from religion to art to philosophy, but their central question is simple: who is better, the lover or the nonlover? Is it better to love or not?

They make their arguments in long speeches, praising each other rapturously for all their well-argued points. Phaedrus begins with his argument in favor of the nonlover, which in essence suggests that love makes you crazy, sick, and unreasonable. He asks Socrates whether a man be right in trusting himself to one "who is *possessed with a malady* which no experienced person would attempt to cure, for the patient himself admits that he is not in his right mind and acknowledges that he is wrong in his mind, but is unable, as he says, to control himself. How, if he came to his right mind, could he imagine that the desires were good which he conceived when in his wrong mind?"[1] Phaedrus describes love like an amoeba that takes control of the lover's body and mind, making him irrational, unhappy, unlikeable. He can't be reasoned with, he makes deleterious decisions, he doesn't attend to his studies, his duties, his health. The lover's life is full of desire, regret, jealousy, distraction. The lover is obsessed with the object of love, always wondering where she is, and if she is being unfaithful. He is *lovesick*, and lovesickness goes to your head, causing a pleasurable, addictive madness so that you cannot trust yourself. To be friends with a *lovesick person* is a stressful and tumultuous experience, an observation with which anyone who has supported a friend through a toxic relationship can relate.

The non-lover, on the other hand, says Phaedrus, has no such troubling dilemmas. "The non-lover has no such tormenting recollections; he has never neglected his affairs or quarrelled with his relations; he has no troubles to reckon up, or excuses to allege; for all has gone smoothly with him." Phaedrus finds life much easier when not bothered by all these evils, commending friendship in place of romantic love. Friends have your best in mind, Phaedrus argues, while lovers seem bent on making your own (and their!) life difficult and damaging: "You are likely to be improved by me, whereas the lover will spoil you."[2] Phaedrus comes to the reasonable conclusion that love is simply not worth it. He ends his oration by advocating that sensible people will just stay in the friend zone—less messy!

Socrates praises Phaedrus for his convincing speech, and for the most part he concedes his points. Yes, love does drive you mad; yes, it would be more convenient and less complicated to commend the non-lover. Love is a madness, a sickness; it makes us unreasonable and is hazardous. And yet, for all this, Socrates still thinks that love is worth it, necessary even, for the destiny of the soul. The soul, Socrates claims, is not destined to merely be content in itself; it derives its essence from the forms (something like God in Plato) and finds its fulfillment in returning to the forms. Love, claims Socrates, when it is purified of base desire for pleasure, pulls the soul out of itself and toward the forms; love is a madness, yes, but it is a divine madness.

In one of the most memorable images in ancient philosophy, Socrates describes the soul as being ruled by two kinds of love: the unruly desire for earthly pleasure and a true love for the good. He imagines them like two horses yoked together, difficult to corral. And yet, if the good horse can win out over the base desires of the bad, then much is possible. Plato, speaking through his imagined Socrates, writes, "When a soul is perfect and has its wings, it travels through the sky and takes part in the governance of the entire cosmos."[3] We are not meant to stay within the circle of our own little needs and necessities indefinitely. The madness of love pulls us out of ourselves, and if we can learn to discipline and direct the unruly desires of the dark horse, it may lead us to the forms, to something like God.

In the end, it seems we are left believing that love is madness, but it is a necessary madness. This description of madness or sickness can be and feel very fitting. "Love" can feel like a stomach flu, the flutters of which we deny before it engrosses all our attention and drains every nutrient, discipline, and vigor from our lives. And when it seeks us out, there's almost nothing we can do other than suffer it and try to minimize its symptoms, its consequences.

When I read Socrates' description of the lover driven mad, who neglects his obligations and quarrels with his family, I can see people I have known who have driven their life to destruction. I am not much of a scientist, but what little I know about the chemistry of infatuation is that it is like a drug, a sickness, or if you wanted to be more imaginative about it, a magic spell—very difficult to break. It is perhaps no wonder that many in my generation have chosen to, as Socrates puts it, prefer the non-lover to the lover. But as Socrates artfully lays out, even the madness of love can be a good thing when it leads us out of ourselves.

There is something beautiful about the way love takes over; it is a madness, yes, a catching sickness. But it can draw us out of the safe circle of what we know. This is beautifully illustrated in George Eliot's remarkable little book *Silas Marner*. We avoid the madness of love for all kinds of reasons, many of which merit not judgment but tenderness, which Eliot illustrates so mercifully in her book. It tells the story of Silas Marner, a man who takes solace in his little pile of gold money that he has collected, using work as a way to keep living after a deep betrayal by his religious community.

It is only when his pile of gold is mysteriously replaced by the golden curls of a child, seemingly abandoned, that he begins to heal. In loving another little human, in coming to be her caretaker, Silas discovers new possibilities of hope and wholeness. Though this love, in some ways, controls him, it is also the source of his healing. Eliot writes, "He recovered a consciousness of unity between his past and present. The sense of presiding goodness and the human trust that comes with all pure peace and joy had given him a dim impression that there had been some error, some mistake that had thrown that dark shadow over the days of his best years."[4]

As Silas comes to love the little golden curls instead of his pile of gold, he learns (and teaches us) the meaning of Jesus' words "Where your treasure is, there your heart will be also" (Matthew 6:21). For Silas, love is something that takes over his life. He becomes *lovesick*, as Plato writes, but it is a divine madness that opens the horizons of his pain and selfishness. Love can be a sickness, and a sickness that leads unto death, but not all death is bad; the death to self can see in its place new life and new vistas.

There is a little word in Jesus' words that catches my eye: *where*. And here we are introduced to one of love's other metaphors. Love can be a madness, but love is not only something that happens to us, not only sickness and madness, even if they be divine. Love is also somewhere we go, something we nurture and look after. Love is also a home.

## Love Is (Not) a Home

I want you to do something. Imagine with me the living room of your childhood home. Or, if like me, you moved around a bit, the room that felt most like home. What was the shape of the room? Where did the light come in? What was your favorite piece of furniture? How did you feel there?

Let me tell you about mine. It is a cozy room, and fairly dark. Windows line the wall to the left of the hearth, but a small door leads out to a covered porch there, so very little natural light comes through their panes. And yes, there is a hearth, not wood burning, mind you, but during the winter its gas flame provides genuine warmth and coziness.

The dog cushion is set immediately in front of the red-brick facade to maximize the coziness. After a long day of barking at squirrels and hiding tennis balls, Darcy, our elderly golden retriever, wanders from person to person, concluding her unsuccessful mission to get petted by curling in a disconsolate semi-circle, her furry little face hanging just over the edge of the bed. She has gotten fat and looks very much like a golden-brown loaf of bread. Those of us from whom she has attempted to obtain pets are draped wearily over the two couches and two overstuffed chairs. One of the couches, with its back against the windowless wall, is of a warm brown leather with brass tacks holding its folds together handsomely. It is more stately, but less comfortable. The cushions of the other couch are misshapen and adorned with tangled tassels. It's infinitely preferable to occupy in the event that you are trying to watch a movie. It is coziness, safety, rest.

One of the metaphors we use when speaking about love and human relationships is home. When we begin to feel comfortable we *open up to someone*, like a door swinging open. When someone resists, we say they *slammed the door* or that *their walls went up*; we don't usually mean a literal door or wall, but rather that they have, rightly or wrongly, put up barriers to intimacy, to closeness, to exchange. One of the ways we might begin to love someone is when we realize that we can *feel at home* with them; one of love's deepest claims is that someone *is home to me*. Love can become a refuge for us in the chaos of the world, a place we can belong.

This is one of the themes that Wendell Berry dwells on in the novel *Hannah Coulter*. The book follows the life of one woman from early life during World War II, through the rapid changes in rural America right up to the turn of the twenty-first century. Hannah marries Nathan Coulter, and a great deal of the book is taken up with their relationship. Hannah (the narrator of the novel) describes their marriage as a "room of love":

> The room of love is another world. You go there wearing no watch, watching no clock. It is the world without end, so small that two people can hold it in their arms, and yet it is bigger than worlds on worlds, for it contains the longing of all things to be together, and to be at rest together. You come together to the day's end, weary and sore, troubled and afraid. You take it all in your arms, it goes away, and there you are where giving and taking are the same, and you live a little while entirely in a gift. The words have all been said, all permissions given, and you are free in the place that is the two of you together. What could be more heavenly than to have desire and satisfaction in the same room?[5]

Nathan Coulter is a man who has seen war, carries its violence in his chest, and wishes for a better life. Hannah also has lost, and as the passage describes they are often "weary and sore, troubled and afraid." But they seek to live a good life, and their labor of loving one another becomes an ongoing practice of "gentleness opposite to . . . war."[6] Hannah speaks of Nathan being "her guest" and she as "his welcomer," or sometimes the other way around, imaging their marriage to each other as an ongoing act of hospitality.[7]

I love the word *homemaking*. For many of us, it might conjure an image either arcane or horrifying, a 1950s housewife with a silicone smile, or a hope chest and a quilt on the prairie with Laura Ingalls. But just think about it for a moment: home-making. Love leads to home-making. I think of this in terms of our individual loves. In contrast to the idea of love as madness, something that happens to us, the idea of love as home-making reminds us that we have agency in the continual cultivation of love.

Each love will look a little different, in the same way that each living room has its own shape, furniture, and peculiarities. Each home of love will have its distinguishing features that cannot be changed, but much flexibility too. We can replace the couch, repaint the walls. Our love is a place we can continue to make comfortable, safe, and rejuvenating for its occupants. Sometimes this means compromise, for the spouse who wants a TV in the living room, or the child who demands a dog. Love is not handed to us on a platter; it is given to us in a room that we can make our own. Love as a home is something that invites both rest and action: the activity of home-making, of keeping up this place that protects and nourishes us both, but also rest, for it is in the safe enclosure of this love that I can be at ease, be known, and be encompassed.

Sometimes when we speak of the home of love, we do not only mean the home we share together, but our own hearts as the space into which we allow (or don't allow) the beloved. The night before He died Jesus said to His disciples, "Anyone who loves me will obey my teaching. My Father will love them, and we will come to them and make our home with them" (John 14:23). Seeking to aid her fellow Carmelite sisters in their prayer life, in her famous text *The Interior Castle* Teresa of Avila describes the soul as a labyrinthine castle in which God chooses to dwell. With companionable and sisterly gentleness, she invites her readers to dive further into their "interior castles." She writes, "Let us imagine, then, that this castle (as I have said) has several mansions, or rooms; some above, some below, and others on the sides, and that in the center of all these is the *principal* room, in which subjects of the greatest secrecy are discussed between God and the soul."[8] Pulled by the love of God into deeper knowledge of the self, Teresa grows in intimacy and closeness with her creator. In loving God, she becomes known to herself; in being known by God she experiences His love more deeply. And this is another aspect of love; not only belonging, but knowing and seeing, and being seen.

## Love Is (Not) a Mirror

The British band The 1975 open their song "Happiness" with these words: "She showed me what love is; I'm acting like I know myself."[9] It is a clever play on words; profundity treated lightly. On one level, the lead singer (Matty Healy) says he's acting as though he himself knows what love is, even though it's as opaque to him as it is to the teenager wading through the murky waters of romance. But there is another meaning we could wring out of this play on words; Healy is acting like he knows *himself*, as if he has a clear vision of his own motivations and desires and character, when those are as murky to him as the mystery of love itself. These questions belong together; if I don't know myself, how can I know my motivations are not selfish, self-destructive, or simply the result of my own needs and traumas?

It's a theme that shows up again and again in the band's oeuvre. In the song entitled "Sincerity Is Scary,"[10] Healy writhes his way through multiple posturing, virtue-signaling verses and choruses about postmodernism and society and drug use and social media before bringing himself to admit that he just wrote the song because he was mad a girl blew him off after a concert. It took all that hot air to blow away the mist that was covering his honest feelings. How can we know what love is when we're acting (falsely) like we know ourselves? But if we don't know ourselves, where would we begin? In one song addressed to God (in whom he ostensibly does not believe), Healy ends by asking, "If I'm lost, then how can I find myself?" nine times.[11]

It is not coincidence, I think, that at the end of First Corinthians, the famous description of love read at weddings innumerable, we have a description of a mirror. What is love? This is the question First Corinthians seems to answer. The passage describes love in action, as if love itself is a personified metaphor: a person is the basis of the metaphor whose qualities are carried over to love, and the chapter tells us the way love would act. We know the list:

Love is patient, love is kind. Love does not envy, it does not boast, it is not proud. It does not dishonor others, it is not self-seeking, it is not easily angered, it keeps no record of wrongs. Love does not delight in evil but rejoices with the truth. It always protects, always trusts, always hopes, always perseveres. Love never fails.

1 Corinthians 13:4–8

Just like the woman in The 1975 song, this passage "shows us what love is." Love acts in ways that are patient, kind, content, humble, and honoring. This is what love looks like, how it acts. And then the passage almost abruptly turns to the metaphor of a mirror: "Now we see only a reflection as in a mirror. . . . Now I know in part; then I shall know fully, *even as I am fully known*" (13:12, italics added). Love has to do not only with seeing and knowing the beloved, but also being seen by them. Just as Matty Healy's lover helps him "know himself," it is in seeing love, and experiencing it, that we begin to truly know ourselves. In earthly love, we are offered a mirror, a clearer view of ourselves, but someday we will see through this dark glass as though it is a window; in loving we will not only see a reflection of our own needs and desires but truly be able to behold the beloved, and to be beheld.

The poet and artist William Blake once wrote that "the most sublime act is to set another before you."[12] To love someone is to stand before the mystery and terror of another human being, their need and blessedness and woundedness, to not only see, but *behold*. When I think of the word *behold*, I think not only of the act of sight, but of the posture of attention, of honor, of witness. In Romanticism, sublimity came to be a complex concept bound up with nature and the divine. Though its definition is contested, its basic sense is this: beauty and terror. To behold and be beheld is both a terrifying and a beautiful thing, but the closest, it seems, we can get to being like God.

## Show Me What Love Is

In many of the ways that we speak about love, we tend to describe ourselves in some kind of passive role: we fall in love, it happens to us, and we live in the light of this thing we cannot help. In a way, there is a truth to this. We do not generate love in ourselves. It is a gift that we receive and, throughout the course of our lives, learn to reciprocate. We learn the patterns of love and tenderness from our parents, receiving as tiny babies love we cannot earn but simply merit by our existence. The ways we relate and know how to love are because we were taught by our parents, by our siblings, by other people who showed us love in life. We are sometimes capable of great love, greater than our fractured experiences should allow, but perhaps that is because woven into our very being is the parent-love of God, of whom the apostle John writes, "We love because he first loved us" (1 John 4:19). In that sense, love is something that happens to us, something we experience.

But a great share of the pleasure of meaningful relationships is not only being loved, but getting to love in return. As children grow and develop, they begin to want to love, to have relationships, and to give gifts as their parents do. This is not a loss, a dull dredging into an era of the responsible life in which one no longer receives but gives. No, being able to practice the art of love, to respond generously to the love that has been shown to us, that is one of life's great privileges, one of the great honors of being a human.

The metaphors in this chapter give me a way to imagine actively taking on the mantle of love. Love as a madness inspires me to be willing to be felled by love, to let it take over my life and make demands of me. In that loss of myself, I see the beginning of true life. It is a reminder that "whoever wants to save their life will lose it, but whoever loses their life . . . will save it" (Matthew 10:39). I pray that

I can see this sickness, this madness as the beginning of real life, that, like Socrates' charioteer, I can learn to discipline those selfish and darker impulses, so that love might meet its mark.

In the metaphor of love as a house, I remember that I can make myself hospitable to others, that my love relationships are not static, but ongoingly cultivated. That every year, every week, every day, I can see what needs repair in this house, how I might make it more suited to the both of us, how I might make it safe, warm.

Love as a mirror makes me hope that on the dark days of the people I love, I will clean my own vision enough so that in me, they would see reflected not my own needs and desires of who I'd like them to be, but their own image, beloved by God, precious and good. And I pray that in my halting attempts at love, I may begin to know myself what love is.

 ## LIVING, THINKING, PRAYING

Love is patient, love is kind. It does not envy, it does not boast, it is not proud. It does not dishonor others, it is not self-seeking, it is not easily angered, it keeps no record of wrongs. Love does not delight in evil but rejoices with the truth. It always protects, always trusts, always hopes, always perseveres.

Love never fails. But where there are prophecies, they will cease; where there are tongues, they will be stilled; where there is knowledge, it will pass away. For we know in part and we prophesy in part, but when completeness comes, what is in part disappears. When I was a child, I talked like a child, I thought like a child, I reasoned like a child. When I became a man, I put the ways of childhood behind me. For now we see only a reflection as in a mirror; then we shall see face to face. Now I know in part; then I shall know fully, even as I am fully known.

And now these three remain: faith, hope and love. But the greatest of these is love.

1 Corinthians 13:4–13

### ▧ LIVING METAPHORS

Think of your childhood home, or the place that you feel most at home in the world. What does it look like? What are the colors on the walls? The pieces of decoration you most cherish? What are the textures and materials of the room? How do they feel? Imagine touching a blanket or a chair, or perhaps the warm body of a family pet. What smells remind you of home? The strong yet cozy smell of black coffee from an early bird parent, a pizza in the oven?

Now think of a friendship in which you feel at home. What are the qualities of that relationship? In what ways do being loved and feeling at home with that person mirror the place you feel at home?

### ▧ THINKING AND PRAYING

*Poem*: "Those Winter Sundays," Robert Hayden
*Painting*: *The Banjo Lesson* (1893), Henry Ossawa Tanner
*Film*: *The Painted Veil* (2006)
*Poem*: "Love III," George Herbert

In Hayden's poem we are offered a poignant portrait of love, that of a father who shows rather than speaks love, attention shown through the "austere and lonely offices" of love. We tend to think of love as a warm and soft thing; Hayden's depiction of love is, quite literally, cold as he describes a father rising early to warm the house. This profound but not frilly poem honors the upraised, unrelenting faithfulness that a deep love can offer.

Tanner's *The Banjo Lesson* depicts a less stern image of love in the gently guiding hands of a grandparent. The grandfatherly figure embraces but does not enclose the child in his lap, watching with care but not disturbing the searching fingers of the experimenting musician, an image with a gravity purposefully undermining the racist minstrel stereotypes of Tanner's time. This simple image can itself act as a metaphor of love: to teach someone can be a form of love, to show them the way, but to let them explore without control.

For most of us, learning to love is learning what love is not, allowing our expectations to be upset, broken, and remade, like the spouses in *The Painted Veil*. The movie is a metaphor of the ways in which we hide from each other and obscure our true selves. The film follows the slow and painful process of two selfish people learning to be hospitable to each other, graciously mending in and with each other what they have mutually broken.

The same loving hospitality is at the heart of George Herbert's magnificent poem. Herbert offers a mixed, or perhaps more appropriately, melded, metaphor in which love (who is Christ) is both the host of the feast and the feast itself. Here, there is a double meaning, host as one who welcomes others into their home, and host as a word to describe the bread of the eucharist. Christ, then, is pictured as welcoming us to a table at which we do not feel worthy to sit, and yet where we find the satisfaction for our deep hunger for love.

# CREATION
## IS (NOT)
# BIRTH

The whole creation has been groaning as in the pains of childbirth right up to the present time.

Romans 8:22

*Adioro te infans si es masculus an femina, per Patrem et Filium et Spiritum sanctum, ut exas et recedas, et ultra ei non noceas neue inspipientam illi facias.*

A childbirth charm, from British Library<br>manuscript Junius 8[1]

**M**y first niece was born in the middle of a wild snow-storm, the most severe the United Kingdom had seen in thirty years. The trains slid to a stop, and most of the shops closed. While my sister labored on the other side of the border from Scotland, I tossed and turned in bed, a nervous wreck the whole night long. I was worried about everything: whether my sister would make it to the hospital, whether she'd endure the birth safely, whether the baby would be okay. *We live in modern times,* I told myself. *Yes, modern times with hospitals and precautions,* I reassured. *Things are much safer than they used to be.* But thumping in every vein of my body was a primal fear. *There is still so much that can go wrong, that does go wrong,* I rejoined. Fear of childbirth runs deep in my bones, as deep as our exile from Eden: "In pain you shall bring forth children" (Genesis 3:16 ESV). And in pain and peril we still do.

But then she was born. Lilian Joy, a brand-new human, barely a breath old and loved more than she will ever understand. Our world wrapped itself in a cloak of cozy jubilation. The clothes laid out were donned; the pacifiers accomplished their work of pacifying; meals prepared for the nursing mother were eaten. And in those first visits, we tentative new uncles and aunts held our fragile and wonderfully alive new relative. New life prepared for, and then received in a flurry of love and practicalities. With my sister's other births, I still found myself holding my breath, releasing it in relief only to have it taken away again at the wonder of an entirely new person in the world, reaching with curious hands and searching gray eyes.

Birth is one of the ways we speak about thought, creativity, and vocation; about undertaking work that might change us. In these metaphors sometimes *we are the ones giving birth*, and other times we are the one *to whom birth is being given*. We *conceive of* a new idea. A change has *given birth* to a new set of circumstances, an artistic work of art, a political movement. Something someone said was *pregnant*; we mean it was loaded down with unspoken (unborn) meaning that might change everything. An artist *labors* over her painting. A musician is *reborn* after years in retirement. The ways that we use this metaphor can allow us to see creativity and vocations not as things that merely happen to us, but as things we can approach mindfully and bravely.

## Birth Is Hard Work

When I was in the throes of writing my PhD thesis, I used a mixed metaphor to describe the painful process of drafting each new chapter: giving birth and carving marble. These metaphors seemed given to me, natural in their own right, rather than chosen or crafted. This was how I imagined the process of approaching a new chapter in my project: when I *conceived* of the direction for a new chapter in my thesis, it began with *a seed* of *an idea* in my mind, a vague *concept* of where I would begin. While it was still in this *embryonic* stage, I fed the idea on books, articles, and conversations, allowing it to *grow* and *take shape* as it was nourished by my formal and informal research, meditation, and discussions. Sometimes, feeling particularly inspired, I would have a desire to begin writing, but I would stop, pause, held back by an intuitive sense that the idea needed *a little more time to gestate*. And then, in the fullness of time, the urge to write came and I obeyed it.

Thus began the protracted, painful process of getting the darn thing on the page. I have always found writing difficult. Of course, there are moments of flow and pleasure in the process, but every project I have really been proud of has required periods of unbearable tedium, *laboring* over a single sentence, *pushing through* one paragraph after another, wondering if at some point I would simply run out of the capacity to continue, unable to *bear* such monotonous agony. But then, there it is!

There is always an element of surprise when the thing finally presents itself to me through the work of my *laboring* fingers. I look at the first draft: "There you are! Just as I imagined, and different." And of course, just because the thing is on the page doesn't mean it is finished. This is where the second metaphor comes in. I have birthed a piece of marble. Now that it is in the world and the raw material is there before me, the statue itself can begin to be found within the rough form of marble, finer details hewn out of its roughness, language polished, rough arguments smoothed. The metaphorical mixing is, I will admit, not pleasing, but there is no accounting for these things. Giving birth to a block of marble seems neither safe nor pleasant, but then neither is completing a thesis. Having mothered forth the idea, I needed only to raise it.

The world of thought is often connected with birth, genealogy, and lineage. My mixed metaphor came naturally, not through any ingenuity of my own, but because it is one of the systems of idioms we use to describe something moving from the realm of *thought* and manifesting in the world of what we call *life*. Etymologically, *conceive* and *conception* can be associated with becoming pregnant or forming an idea in your mind.

In philosophy, the word *genealogy* has been used to trace the *lineage* of ideas, as though an idea that Aristotle *generated* might be inherited throughout the generations.[2] Taking this approach, some philosophers attempt to trace the *DNA* of *concepts* through different articulations of words and ideas over history and contexts. This technical use of *genealogy* and my own imposition of the idea of the *DNA* here are in themselves metaphorical, transposing the original sense of *genealogy*: a family tree (another tree metaphor!).

Just as the gospels of Matthew and Luke trace Jesus' ("The Word" as John would say) lineage through the patriarchs and brave mothers of the Hebrew Bible, thinkers who engage in philosophies of genealogy trace the lineage of words and ideas. Ideas have not only parents, but families, generations of passing down not a clone but an offspring of similar *concepts* and phrases, which takes a slightly different form in every generation, but whose branches can be traced back to a father (or mother) root. People are trees, and so are ideas. And we naturally speak of ideas as *giving birth* to movements, objects, and passions in the "real world." We say that the ideas of Karl Marx *gave birth* to the Bolshevik revolution, or that desire "gives birth to sin" (James 1:15).

The way we speak about ideas seems to imply that they long to be given a form, a body in the world. This can be connected not only to writing and the lineage of ideas, but of the process of creativity: of imagining something, and then bringing it to life. In *Walking on Water*, her meditation on Christian artistry, Madeleine L'Engle uses the metaphor to describe the process of an artist bringing a work of art to life, of the movement from *idea* to *form*. She writes:

> I believe that each work of art, whether it is a work of great genius or something very small, comes to the artist and says, "Here I am. Enflesh me. Give birth to me." And the artist either says, "My soul doth magnify the Lord," and willingly becomes the bearer of the work, or refuses; but the obedient response is not necessarily a conscious one, and not everyone has the humble, courageous obedience of Mary.[3]

L'Engle describes the process of *having an idea* for a work of art and bringing it to life as a process of birth; conceiving, bearing, and birthing. The ideas of a philosopher grow in a lineage of thought, and the work of art is given birth through the artist's consent. But what of other endeavors?

## Birth Is (Not) a Calling

What L'Engle describes seems to be not only the process of creating something but the vocation (or what we might call the "calling") of the artist. In its oldest usage, *vocation* had to do with spiritual callings to the priesthood. The language of calling is ingrained in the word, which shares its origins with *vocal*. In certain Christian traditions, *vocation* has a very strong definition in relationship to marriage: you are called either to a vocation of marriage or to consecrated singleness (in either the priesthood, religious life, or a godly single layperson's life). These callings have a similar shape: someone is called to the priesthood (or the religious life), and they respond to the call through their vows. Someone is called to marriage, and they answer through vows.

This idea of vocation resonates in the way that L'Engle speaks about the artist. Artists are called and they answer. She imagines them like Mary at the annunciation. The Gospel of Luke gives us the account that has come to be called the annunciation. An angel visits Mary, a young and unmarried woman, and tells her she is to bear the Messiah. In one of the most significant moments in all of Christian history, Mary answers this call, this vocation, with the words: "May your word to me be fulfilled" (Luke 1:38). This has come to be known as Mary's *fiat*, the Latin word used in the Vulgate translation of the passage, meaning "let it be done." Mary is addressed, she is called, and she answers the call. She "willingly became the bearer of the work" of redemption.

The poet Denise Levertov attaches the annunciation not merely to artistic or priestly vocations, but to those significant moments of decision and calling in our lives. In her poem "Annunciation," Levertov connects that moment of Mary's own calling to the significant moments in our own lives when we are offered a choice: to marry, to move, to respond to a calling.[4] Our moments of calling are rarely so dramatic. Angels do not usually visit us. Often, those moments of decision happen somewhere seemingly inconsequential: over a lunch when we begin to realize that we love someone, on the commute to work in the form of an email telling us we've been accepted to a program overseas, the tugging in our hearts while watching a priest offer the eucharist, the thought, *I'd like to help serve this feast.* In these moments we are called out to and asked, "Will you do this? Will you marry this woman? Will you be a priest of God? Pour yourself into this cause?" Are you willing to say yes to this thing, this person, to *bear* it, and *labor* over it? To bring this stirring inside you into the world?

To say yes to a calling is to agree to bear consequences that you cannot yet imagine. One of the things about giving birth, I'm told, is that you can't quite imagine what it will be like until it happens. On the one hand, you can't imagine how much it will hurt and the manifold ways in which it will hurt, but you also can't imagine how much love will flood the valleys and caves of your life. I heard one mother put it this way: "I never knew that so many people were walking around like this, so full of an overwhelming, almost violent love."

When I was admitted to my doctoral program, my supervisor looked at me over an untouched latte and said, "Today we will celebrate and be excited about your admission, but on another day we will talk about how this will be harder than you think and will require more of you than you can imagine. You do not have to do this; you can do something else with your life." It was an annunciation moment for me; it was a calling to which I could say either yes or no. And I chose to say yes. I could not see then how much it would require of me, and I still can't see the fullness of the consequences of saying yes.

But there are deeper vocations, ones that get closer to the bone of what it is to be human. Marriage too is a vocation.

Someone says to another, "Do you want to marry me?" The very nature of marriage is that we must answer this question before knowing what the answer will mean. We cannot anticipate how much it will require of us, who it will help us become.

People can say no to their callings. If a proposal of marriage is to be legitimate, it must anticipate the real possibility of a refusal. There are many good reasons to say no to a calling, or even, I think, to bargain with it (though, beware, if Moses, Abraham, and Zechariah are any example, such an approach rarely goes well in an uncomplicated way).

Sometimes people undertake grand destinies begrudgingly, out of obligation, so the sheer elation of choice is never enjoyed. But as Levertov notes with devastating clarity, this is not usually how vocations are avoided; more often they are turned away from with dread, in weakness, but followed by a sense of relief, not regret. Binding yourself to one person, with all their hidden and unhidden sins, for life is a terrifying thing. Bearing the cross of priesthood one's entire life is no light thing. Making your body and then your life the home for a new human being in a broken world is an almost irrational, irresponsible thing to do. Moments of calling usually happen in private, over dinner, in an email, during a quiet moment of prayer that no one else observes. Often no one else will know if we did not answer the call of a vocation. And yet, there is tragedy in that. We carry on with our lives. Lightning doesn't fall from the sky. But the question has been answered, the path turned away from, not to be faced again.[5]

The first time I read this poem, it had a great effect on me. First, I felt my old fear of missing out: I do not want to miss the pathway. But then something more essential, and, I hope, mature arose. I realized that I wanted to be a person who was ready to say yes when those personal moments of annunciation came to me. I didn't want to turn away; I didn't want to be a coward. If we are to live meaningful lives, we must find a way to answer the callings, the vocations that wait in store for our *fiat*.

But these are weighty things. I sometimes wonder if the decline in marriage in my own generation is not out of a disrespect of marriage, but out of a sense of its high calling, and out of the trauma of growing up in a generation whose parents have unprecedented divorce rates. It is not that we don't want to be married, or that we do not value marriage, but that we are afraid of failing at it. We are apprehensive. Of course, we are. And we've seen many other shatterings of vocation too. Disgraced pastors, corrupt leaders, failed artists. We turn away from vocations not in apathy, but in despair.

Many things will call to you in life, and you need not answer them all. But to never answer is a loss. To never give yourself to a great work, the creation of a work of art, the love of a person, the bearing of a child, the limitations of a call to ministry—that too is a loss. Life is made meaningful by the things we say yes to, even though we can't see to what end those things will lead.

I think each of us knows when something is a real, deep calling. When we find ourselves in the presence of something that calls us to deep creativity, to long faithfulness, we can remember the example of Mary, in her solicitude and decision. My image of Mary is one of empowered consent. She listened, she "pondered these things in her heart" (see

Luke 2:19), she responded to the call on her life. In answering the call, she not only agreed to undertake a task, but she became something she was not before: the Mother of our Lord. With great change comes fear, crisis even. This too is birth.

## Birth Is (Not) Death

In her poem "Metaphors," hastily written on an evening when she mistakenly came to the conclusion she was pregnant, Sylvia Plath ends her recitation of metaphors for pregnancy (bread in an oven, a giant watermelon) with the ominous proclamation that she "boarded the train there's no getting off."[6] The strange thing about birth is that there comes a time where it simply must happen, for baby and mother. You can't wait any more. You can't decide you'd rather not go through with it. A baby must leave the mother if either is to survive. And it is about survival.

Birth and death are neighbors; they haunt each other, never letting one forget the other. In the same hospital where old, diseased, destroyed lungs rattle out their last breath, fragile rib cages expand to greet the world with a shriek. In her book *Childbirth as a Metaphor for Crisis*, Claudia Bergmann observes that in Scripture and in the textual tradition of the ancient near east there was a tradition of comparing women giving birth to men going into battle.[7] Once you've entered battle, you must find a strategy, be it hiding or fighting, for you will soon die if you do not. While Plath's metaphor of a train is more domestic, there is an element that links these metaphors for birth: once the thing has started, there's no going back. Once you're on a train, it will go where it will go. A part of what frightens us about this moment of crisis is not only whether or not we will survive, but who we will become after we've survived. In giving birth to a baby, a mother is also born.

Some time ago, I found myself thirty thousand feet in the air over a pillowing of clouds, struggling to catch my breath. I often find myself feeling very existential on airplanes, and on that day I found it to be particularly so because I had just been offered a wonderful and terrifying possibility. It was a vocational moment: a question had been posed, a calling out I longed to say yes to, but one which in the face of, I found myself frozen with fear. But I said yes, I "boarded the train," as Plath puts it. It was the most joyful thing I have ever done. And yet in that season all I could do was prepare and wait. It was like I was weaving my own chrysalis, gasping for air as the threads began to close over the life that I had known. I couldn't step out of the chrysalis now. It was very, very good. And I could have screamed.

As I flew, I listened to Ólafur Arnalds' other-worldly *some kind of peace*, which is mostly instrumental. But as I stared nervously over the canopy of clouds, contemplating all that was to come, the final track came on, which features a spoken monologue by the folk singer Lhasa de Sala.[8] In it, she describes the experience of birth from the perspective of the baby. She describes the warmth and ease of the womb and imagines how apocalyptic it must feel to be a baby being born, pushed out of the warm closeness of a mother into the world, and yet how necessary it is. There is a moment when a baby must be born, when the womb becomes cramped. The change must come and it will be life-giving, but it must feel like the end of the world for the baby. She begins to make it a metaphor for death, that there will come a moment for all of us where we must leave the womb of this world, where we are, as she puts it, "obliged to be born." It is good, and terrifying.

As I listened, I began to see myself not merely as Mary answering the call to bear Christ; I was also the baby undergoing birth. And I realized that not only was I afraid of birth, but of being given birth to. It was like I'd been in the womb all this time, and I couldn't imagine what my life after birth could mean. With ascent to a vocation comes an enrichment in identity: the women who bears a child is always thereafter a mother. The man who marries is ever thereafter a husband. The person who makes vows is a priest forever. This shift in identity can feel like (and perhaps is) a kind of death of our previous self, so comfortable and known to ourselves. And that can be terrifying. We fear not only what life will be like with this new baby, new marriage, new calling, but also who we will become. It feels wonderful, but also disorienting and frightening, like a kind of death.

Perhaps this was what Nicodemus felt when he came to Jesus in the cover of darkness. Nicodemus was an important man, with a reputation to preserve, people who counted on him. This important man came to Jesus, a preacher, a prophet, or a problem, depending on who you asked. Why did he come? Was it to test Jesus? To probe his orthodoxy and give a report? His opening words, according to the Gospel of John, are simply: "Rabbi, we know that you are a teacher who has come from God. For no one could perform the signs you are doing if God were not with him" (3:2). Not a question, a statement. Was it one he really believed, or one he merely tried out to see how Jesus would answer?

Jesus' answer is strange; to me it seems to be a non sequitur: "Very truly I tell you, no one can see the kingdom of God unless *they are born again*" (3:3, italics added).

Nicodemus speaks of miracles, and Jesus answers with the initial, fundamental miracle that brings us out into the world: birth. Nicodemus asks the obvious question: "How can someone be born when they are old?" (3:4). John doesn't give us the tone in which this is written. Is it earnest curiosity? Is it playful mocking, a gentle resistance to the poetry of the popular preacher? Or is it spoken with the understated intensity of someone who feels that they are about to enter into the womb as an old man, one who feels it is already happening, one who is terrified and waiting to be born?

The answer Jesus gives is as mysterious as His first—an answer full of poetry: wind blowing here and there and being heard, heaven and heavenly things, snakes being lifted up (3:5–8, 10–15). But at the heart of it is the *necessity of being born again*. This interaction is the one that prompts the apostle John to write perhaps some of the best-known words in the Bible: "For God so loved the world that he gave his one and only Son, that whoever believes in him shall not perish but have eternal life" (3:16). This is the greatest moment of calling, the voice that calls every human being: the call from death to life. This is the great vocation of all human existence, to be drawn into the loving life of God, to not perish, but to live. And the way is through birth. We are, once and for all, obliged to be born.

The clouds parted as we began to descend, and I felt the fluttering butterflies in my belly begin to make a landing of their own, no longer turning my stomach over in fearfulness. In the quiet mystery of the clouds, where normal life seems almost not to exist, I did find, as the title of Ólafur Arnalds' album implies, *some kind of peace*. In the period leading up to that moment, I had connected my experience to that of Mary, being called out to, asked, giving her consent. But in the air, I began to see my experience as connected with, first, Nicodemus, who seemed afraid of being born, just like I was. But then also, I realized, to Jesus, the God of the universe, the "firstborn over all creation" (Colossians 1:15), who consented to be born. In the dark of the night, I went, like Nicodemus, to Jesus, and I found that I too needed to be born again. But in that birth, I was not alone, as Nicodemus wasn't. The God who so loved the world that He gave himself was with me.

## Consent Illumined Her

Responding to the call of a vocation is a difficult and frightening thing and should be undertaken with seriousness appropriate to the calling. I love the words of the Introduction to the marriage ceremony in the *Book of Common Prayer*, which says marriage "is not by any to be . . . taken in hand, unadvisedly, lightly, or wantonly . . . but reverently, discreetly, advisedly, soberly, and in the fear of God; duly considering the causes for which Matrimony was ordained."[9] We should approach those questions of vocation in our life with gravity, but not with so much fear that we never find it in ourselves to say yes. These moments of calling can feel too much for us, because they are; it is weighty and terrifying to say yes to a vocation, be it marriage or the work of the religious life, but it is also the threshold of great potential growth. It is an essentially human thing that our choices in life can affect the world, that God involves us in the shaping of the world through our own consent. But consent is not control; there is much we cannot know, even as we say yes to the vocation before us.

When facing vocational questions, I have found it helpful to meditate on the African American painter Henry Ossawa Tanner's painting *The Annunciation* (1898). It was painted during a period in his work where he was fascinated with present-day Palestine, the land of Jesus' birth. Unlike the highly symbolic annunciations of the Middle Ages, with their lecterns and books situated in what appear to be monasteries where a ponderous Virgin looks to be in her forties, Tanner's depiction is humble, warm, earthy. Mary is the age she probably would have been (early teens), sitting in a room of warm oranges and reds and greens and browns. The angel appears to her as a beam of light. Mary gazes at the beam, her hands clasped but not strained. Her head is tilted in evident curiosity; her mouth is pursed, ready, it seems, to ask the question "How can it be?" She sits on the edge of an unmade bed, a stray toe sticking out of her brown (rather than the typical blue) draping. In this image, I see calmness, curiosity, openness, and reserve. She looks at the beam, but her posture is one of circumspection; she has not yet agreed, I do not think. She has not yet consented.

Perhaps my favorite line in Levertov's poem is simply this: "consent illumined her."[10] That is what I see in Tanner's painting. And it is what I want to find in myself. When the moment comes, I want the bravery to say yes. To bear the work of the Spirit within me, and also to be born.

# LIVING, THINKING, PRAYING

I consider that our present sufferings are not worth comparing with the glory that will be revealed in us. For the creation waits in eager expectation for the children of God to be revealed. For the creation was subjected to frustration, not by its own choice, but by the will of the one who subjected it, in hope that the creation itself will be liberated from its bondage to decay and brought into the freedom and glory of the children of God.

We know that the whole creation has been groaning as in the pains of childbirth right up to the present time. Not only so, but we ourselves, who have the firstfruits of the Spirit, groan inwardly as we wait eagerly for our adoption to sonship, the redemption of our bodies. For in this hope we were saved. But hope that is seen is no hope at all. Who hopes for what they already have? But if we hope for what we do not yet have, we wait for it patiently.

Romans 8:18–25

## LIVING METAPHORS

Have you ever anticipated the birth of a baby, whether it was your own or someone else's? Think about the excitement of that experience—the guessing which parent the baby would more closely resemble, the wonder of a new being existing in the world. Think also of the fear associated with that new life—whether the mother and baby would be okay. Think also about the way in which, though it feels like a completion, the baby's arrival is merely the beginning.

## ▦ THINKING AND PRAYING

*Dance*: Rite of Spring, Igor Stravinsky
*Novel*: *Laurus*, Eugene Vodolazkin
*Film/Music*: "Lemonade" (2016) Visual Album,
   Beyoncé
*Painting*: *The Birth of Venus* (1480s), Sandro Botticelli

In the remarkable passage from Romans, the redemption of all creation is pictured as a woman in labor pains, prepared to give birth. Christians groan with creation, Paul writes, both desiring the redemption that will come while experiencing the anguish and fear that comes with birth.

Birth as a powerful symbol of transformation is evident in Igor Stravinsky's *Rite of Spring*. In this strange, sometimes disturbing achronological ballet, Stravinsky imagines a pre-Christian Russia, and how they would have thought about the new life and change that come with spring. The pagan dance is violent, a strange melding of the imagery of sacrifice and birth typical of fertility religions. Reflecting on the difference between this imagery of transformation and the imagery of Christianity is interesting. How do they converge? How do they differ? What role does birth play in both?

*Laurus* is a book about identity and suffering, and its main character is "reborn" four times, represented by the four different names he takes on during the course of the book. The chain of rebirths begins with a traumatic real birth, the fallout of which the main character feels responsible for. (Warning: this book is not for the faint of heart, or those who may be disturbed by a description of a traumatic birth.) What follows is a story of ongoing transformation that traces the subtle difference between self-creation and response to vocation, to that which is stable in our lives and that which is as subject to change as the seasons. With each recreation, the protagonist is invited to respond to the name he is called, not knowing who that name will make him become, a powerful image of the tension between identity and calling, birth as death and also as life.

Beyoncé's striking visual album begins in a womb. The album is about transformation, the breaking of a curse, and fundamentally, it is about marriage. In interviews (and within the album itself) Beyoncé explores the idea of inherited brokenness—in family, in society. However, even as she reckons with the broken things in her own past and in the past of America that contributed to the disintegration of her marriage, in the triumphant "All Night" Beyoncé turns to her once-unfaithful husband and asks him to help her give birth, a vivid picture of the rebirth of their relationship, a breaking of the curse of infidelity that has hung over their family for generations. The album begins in the womb of Beyoncé's fear and ends with the birth of her sorrow, transformed and healed. The process of this birth is fraught, terrifying, a crisis, but its conclusion is new life, transformation, hope. To change and to heal, sometimes we must "enter into the womb a second time"; though it may be frightening and unsure, it is where new life begins.

# SADNESS
## IS (NOT)
# HEAVY

Give your burdens to the Lord, and he will take care of you. He will not permit the godly to slip and fall.

Psalm 55:22 NLT

Instead of the cross, the Albatross
About my neck was hung.

Samuel Taylor Coleridge,
*The Rime of the Ancient Mariner*

nce, I brought my microphone to work with me. As a part of my job, I record interviews with scholars and artists. To ensure good audio quality I use a portable USB mic. The adjective *portable* is, I think, misleading. It is portable in the sense that it is not a studio mic—it is not five feet tall, and it does not need a mixing box or long, snaky cables. But in all other respects, one can hardly describe it as portable. To me, iPhones, cereal bars, and books of less than 300 pages are portable. Even very small dogs can be portable. Bricks, to my mind, are not worthy of the description, and my mic is about the size of a brick, and somehow heavier. But I had two important interviews, so I placed the mic in my backpack, which sagged resentfully, and set off on my daily commute.

At first, I didn't really notice it, except that my usual clip to the train station was slightly slower. Gradually, it began to make ordinary tasks not only more wearying but more complicated. As I pulled my computer in and out of my bag, I was conscious of its lumpy presence. When I went to store my water bottle in the compartment, I felt a twinge of anxiety more than usual (packing a water bottle is always an occasion for some anxiety). And navigating the postage-stamp-sized coffee shop I insist on frequenting became a veritable feat of acrobatics, requiring contorting myself in an effort not to knock people with my bulging burden.

Because I usually used the compartment I was storing the microphone in for the various items I somehow collected throughout the day (books from the library, letters from my office pigeonhole, a small bear I felt it necessary to purchase for my nephew), I found myself carrying random items in my hands, rendering me clumsier than I usually would be, holding items under my arm while I searched for my public transit card, dropping a book, and then a scarf. Sighing.

It slowed me down too. As I attempted to hurry myself toward the train platform on my return, I found myself unable to keep up a light jog with ease, my chest heaving in a fruitless effort to draw in more oxygen. By the time I exited the train on my walk home, my shoulders ached from the weight of it, and as I sat down to dinner the ache moved from my right shoulder blade into my neck and up the side of my head into a tension headache. I had intended to stay up reading, but, somehow, as little a thing as lugging a microphone around London had rendered me exhausted.

In my life, I have sometimes carried another heavy thing around with me all day. This unwieldy weight is technically portable too, but instead of settling as a lumpy burden in my backpack, it dissipates itself throughout my whole body, moving sometimes here and sometimes there. In the morning it settles in my arms and legs, so that getting out of bed requires a great deflating effort, and I am already tired when almost nothing has happened. Each movement—the buttoning of my blouse, the pulling back of my hair—requires concentration and strength I find hard to summon, as if I have sand in my fingers and elbows. When I shut the door behind me, each step feels as though I have concrete in the soles of my shoes. But I proceed.

Over the course of the morning, the weight moves from my shoes into my belly, like a rock in the hollow of my stomach, so that I am not hungry. All day the weightiness moves around: my feet, my back, my neck, even my collar bone sometimes feels like it might break. Maneuvering the world with this load makes everything more complicated. I worry that it will come into contact with something else that I value and damage it: work, friendships, romance, even hobbies might become too much to bear simultaneously.

Sometimes I feel angry, exasperated. I wish I could expel the mass from my body, like a case of food poisoning. That in one violent motion I could rid myself of the misery. This thought seems to make me lighter for a moment, but then the heaviness returns and with it a deep exhaustion. I try not to let the burden get in other people's ways, and I sometimes worry that I am troubling others. I do not want anyone else to carry this shapeshifting heaviness. So I bear it till the day's end and fall into bed depleted, the weight of it pulling me under the waters of a deep and drowning sleep.

This burden has had several names in my life—grief, depression, sadness, disappointment, shame. Carrying around a sadness in your body has much the same effect as carrying around a bulky microphone: it takes up space and energy that you might use for other things; it affects how you move around in the world and what you eat (or cannot eat); it makes you contort yourself so as not to be a burden to other people; it marks things you used to find pleasurable with struggle and discontent. With the decreased margin of sadness, you find yourself less able to handle the normal things of your life, and you are persecuted by a persistent sense of your hands being too full, things being too hard, too much. Perhaps more than anything, you are tired, bone tired, with less energy than normal, exhausted from carrying all day long this heavy burden that people may not see.

In *The Body Keeps the Score*, psychiatrist Bessel van der Kolk makes a comprehensive argument based on extensive research that experiences of trauma leave a residue of damage not only in the mind, but in the body.[1] When we lose someone, we are not only in mental anguish, but we feel our heart, that center of both our physical and emotional being, aches. Feelings like *gut wrench* and *heartbreak* are in some sense literal. We bear them in our body. This is another way of saying that we carry our trauma—and to lesser degrees our sadness, our stress, our loss—in our bodies, just like I carried my mic. Our difficult experiences and our emotional responses to them are *heavy*, they *weigh us down.*

Our language reflects this porous boundary between the physical and emotional burdens we carry. We become *heavyhearted* after hearing tragic news. When we are troubled or sorrowful, we intuitively speak of *carrying burdens,* or wishing that we could *lighten someone's load.* Even the word *depression* carries within it an implication of being weighed or pressed down by a heavy force; we *depress* a lever in a machine, pushing it down under our own weight.

This constellation of metaphors overlaps with those of safety as up and danger as down, or more generally good as up and bad as down. We contrast *low spirits* with *high spirits*, but if we press into the language here, we discover what causes us to be low: heaviness, weightiness, the inability to fly. The opposite of being *heavyhearted* is being *lighthearted*, another version of which is *levity* and its friend *laughter*. One of the pains of *heavyheartedness* is the inability to laugh, to smile, the gravity of sadness pulling the corners of your mouth downward so that even cracking a grin feels wearisome and inauthentic. All the physical indications of sadness are like weights dragging us, a gravitational pull downward. Sad people *stoop* and *hang their heads*; their *countenance falls*. In our language we seem resolved to believe that *sadness is heavy*.

## The Weight of Living

Is sadness heavy or is it a heavy thing? Is there a difference between *emotional heaviness* and *emotional baggage*? We speak of sadness with both of these related metaphors, and I think they make a difference for how we relate to living with sadness.

At any moment during my burdensome day of carrying the portable mic, I could've simply taken the backpack off or thrown the mic into the tracks of the London Underground. In that way, I would've been rid of the burdensome thing that tired me out and made me achy all over. It bears mentioning that the mic would still be heavy, and that I chose to carry the mic. In a manner of speaking, there was always agency involved in the carrying of my burden, always the real possibility of ridding myself of it. Or, hypothetically, I could've simply given the mic to someone else to carry, whether or not they particularly wanted to carry it. I could've left it at an electronics store, or in the staff lounge, or at my best friend's front door. If sadness is like this, a heavy thing, we can get rid of it, put it down, lose it.

But sadness doesn't usually feel this way. It is usually not something outside of us that we can choose to set down. We carry sadness inside us, as something integrally a part of us. Do you wake up one morning and decide to carry a crippling burden into every single one of your interactions? Could you, if you wanted to, simply put that sadness down, smash it with a hammer, or leave it with someone else to look after?

With a sigh, most of us must reluctantly answer that we cannot. Our burdens travel with us, as much a part of us as our skin, our blood, our nails. Our sadness is more like *heaviness in our bones* than a *heavy thing we can set down*. We don't feel we have much of a choice in our sadness. Speaking about sadness as heaviness we can't get rid of is closer to the experience of sadness than sadness as a burden because we can put burdens down, but we can't make a heavy thing any less heavy. It is closer to the undesired but inevitable experience of carrying grief inside us, and the weariness of that.

But we often *do* speak of sadness as a burden rather than heaviness, and perhaps there is something helpful in that. To speak of our sadness as a burden is to externalize it, to make sadness something outside of me. For me, this is a helpful mental trick in thinking about *the nature of my sadness*, thinking of how I can *bear it*. I can't strategize about sand in my veins, but I can think about how to carry a heavy backpack. I can't make my burdens any lighter, but I can decide to set a heavy thing down sometimes, or give it to others. We can't always control the sadnesses that life gives to us, but by thinking of them as a burden that we carry, we can claim more agency over the experience of heaviness and respond to it more actively.

The phrase *emotional baggage* gives us something to think about here. When not used in the context of emotional pain, *baggage* is quite a neutral word. We use it to describe the things we carry with us for travel, usually out of necessity. My microphone was a part of my necessary work baggage. Could I really have simply left the microphone behind? And if I could have, and it was causing me so much frustration, why didn't I? The answer to the first question is that I didn't want to leave the microphone behind, not really. There was a reason I took it with me, and if I left it behind, I would not have been able to complete a task. Furthermore, I could have thrown the microphone into the tracks of an oncoming train, and doing so would've been momentarily relieving, but I also would've lost something that was valuable to me. If I had left it somewhere, in the café or in the hallway of my office building, someone else would have had to clean it up. If I left it with a friend, they would have had to take care of it, and they might come to resent me for not taking care of my own property. So though, yes, I could've set down my microphone anytime, in practice I really couldn't.

I think something similar is true with most of our *emotional baggage*: even if we could get rid of it, we may choose not to. Sadness and other heavy emotions have their work to do. We carry sadness as a testament to the love we have cherished and lost. We carry anger as a persistent demand that justice and goodness should prevail, even though they often don't. It is a stubborn resistance to apathy. To set down these burdens would be to belie the value in what is lost or not present. That is one of the things I find interesting about these burdens we bear, because they are not only invisible, but they are often the burden of absent things. They are the burdens of people we have *lost*, affection we *never received*, desires *unfulfilled* that we have never given up on. We do not carry the person anymore, but the absence of the person. And we do not carry the desired object, but the hollowness of the desire unfulfilled. These absences are whole worlds: the life we thought we would share with someone, decades of experience with a parent we didn't expect to lose, a fuller, happier life with a spouse or partner or a vocation that we can imagine but not obtain. To carry the weight of all that could be or could have been is very heavy. But to set it down? That is to abandon hope and love.

And, in fact, getting rid of our emotional baggage, or luggage, if that makes it more neutral for you, might be irresponsible. I have known many people who, when they couldn't rid themselves of sadness, and felt overwhelmed by it, did their best to ignore it, setting it down in places where it didn't belong, leaving it in the care of their siblings and children, who also became tired and resentful. Often, when we think we are leaving behind heavy emotions, in practice we are actually leaving these burdens for other people to deal with. You have only to ask the child of someone who has sought to ease the pain of grief or anger with alcohol to test this theory, or the child who is living the vicarious life of a parent who chose not to cope—or felt that they simply could not cope—with their own disappointment. The sadness we do not bear and do not address does not often dissipate; it passes into the hands of others—our partners, children, and friends.

Emotions have work to do, and while they are often frustrating and overwhelming, we lose something valuable when we try to rid ourselves of them. If we try to set aside our anger and grief over the injustice perpetrated again and again upon ourselves or others made in the image of

God, we will not have the fuel that drives us to pursue justice. While all these emotions are burdensome, they are also necessary and valuable. We may not be able to rise to the occasion of life if we attempt to rid ourselves of heavy emotions.

I don't think we can live a meaningful life without burdens. We cannot have meaningful relationships without opening ourselves to the *heaviness of grief*. We cannot care about justice, excellence, or beauty in the world without some skin in the game, which often results in disappointment, disillusionment, infuriation. To not feel these things is to not care. The weight of life propels us on the journey toward something; it keeps us planted on the earth, gives direction to our movement and orientation to our action. And even when there is no loss, no deep injustice in our lives, the best of relationships, the most beautiful life has its heaviness, its lifelong obstacles and difficult relationships, its vulnerabilities, its disappointments, its responsibility. The best things in life come with burdens: love, relationships, work, community, belief. Some of these burdens we choose, and some we do not. There is no life without burdens; I don't really want there to be.

Carrying some emotional baggage in life is just a part of the bargain. But what does this mean? Are we all just meant to be sad all the time? And what about those of us who bear undue burdens from our experiences in life—be it from a traumatic childhood or a persistent experience of injustice? Carrying our life luggage feels nearly impossible. What can we do with these heavy things?

Jesus is a master of paradoxes: the mourners who are blessed, the rich who are poor, those who have lost their lives finding them. One of the paradoxes that most arrests my attention is this: light burdens. In one of His most famous teachings Jesus says, "Come to me, all you who are *weary and burdened*, and I will give you rest. Take my yoke upon you and learn from me, for I am gentle and humble in heart, and you will find rest for your souls. For my *yoke is easy* and my *burden is light*" (Matthew 11:28–30, italics added). Here, Jesus uses both *heaviness* and *burdens* to describe the weight of life, and along with it *weariness*, that natural response to carrying heavy things. Jesus too thinks these are heavy things. But what I find so interesting is that Jesus does not promise to take away our burdens; there is, it seems, still a yoke and a burden to bear. We must still carry the *weight of living*. But something about life with Jesus makes burdens more bearable. And we are offered something else too: rest. If Jesus' paradoxical words are faithful (and it will not surprise you to read that I think they are), we can learn to bear them well, with others, through laughter, and with rest.

## Bearing Each Other's Burdens

Galatians 6 says something beautiful: "Carry each other's burdens, and in this way you will fulfill the law of Christ" (Galatians 6:2). *In that way you fulfill the law of Christ*. It's the sort of phrase theologians and biblical scholars love to tie themselves in knots over. What exactly did Paul mean? Is "the law of Christ" an idea he develops elsewhere? Or more deeply in Galatians? From my little research, the phrase seems to be something of an enigma. Paul mentions it once, never defines it, and never uses it again. To my untrained eye, I read in this statement the echoes of the new "commands" that Christ makes as He is preparing to go to His death: "A new command I give you: Love one another. As I have loved you, so you must love one another" (John 13:34). This is the new law: to love, and to love is to take on the burden of others. Or perhaps it means that in the same way that Christ bears the burdens of our sins (which, given His righteousness, are not burdens He should have to bear), we too should carry burdens that aren't ours to carry because we have been shown how to do it, because it has been done for us. Mostly simply, I think we can know that in bearing each other's burdens, in coming alongside each other when what we have to carry is too much for us, we are doing something very holy, something that is close to the heart of what it means to follow Jesus.

Three verses later it says something seemingly contradictory: "each one should carry their own load" (Galatians 6:5). There is a difference between a burden and a load; a load, however heavy and inconvenient, is something we can carry on our own, and should. A merchant must keep all his wares with him in a reasonably portable manner; a pregnant mother may be weary, but she cannot pass her baby to another womb. My load is my load alone. But a burden is different. It is something I might reasonably need help with. If we are to be responsible siblings, partners, parishioners, we must carry our own daily loads, but our inability to carry a burden does not reflect on our strength or godliness; it is simply a fact of life. A boulder will crush you no matter how much you pray or how noble you are.

I hate, *hate* the feeling of being a burden to other people. My first tendency when my overwhelmed feelings urge me to seek support is to ask myself, *Are you just being dramatic?* And don't be mistaken: sometimes I am simply being dramatic. I can't help it; perhaps it is how I came out of the womb, or perhaps simply what life has made of me. Drama exists in me.

I don't want to burden other people, especially if my burden isn't *really* a burden. Or, sometimes, I don't even want other people to *know* I am carrying a heavy thing, because it's embarrassing, or because I am afraid it will make them sad, or because I think, *Suck it up, Joy. You can manage this one on your own.* Sometimes I make my knapsack out to be a boulder. But quite often, and I have come to realize more often than not, I don't. In my life, I have occasionally caused a great deal of misery to other people and myself by trying to bear burdens that were impossible for me to carry alone, collapsing under the weight in a carnage of damage that extended beyond myself to the people who would have happily helped.[2]

If you're pondering these things, I think it is probably a sign that you are bearing a burden, not a load. Don't wait. Something is troubling you, even if it is only the numbness you feel toward life. Put this book down. Go text someone you know will reply. Ask them to coffee, dinner, a walk, a drink. Tell them you've been struggling a bit, and you'd like their perspective and support. And if they don't respond, text somebody else.

If you have a tendency to be both depressed and dysfunctional, and yet somehow incredibly confident about your capacity to make it in the world and profoundly embarrassed by the idea of someone supporting you when you are meant to be the one supporting others, what I am about to

155

say will sound eminently mockable to you, but I want you to read it and take it seriously: in not letting others bear your burdens you are preventing them from the deep joy and calling of fulfilling the law of Christ. To reject others offering to be the love of Christ to you is, in a way, to reject Christ. To be able to bear each other's burdens is a great honor, a holy, dignified thing. To not let other people be Christ to you is to hold a simultaneously very high and low opinion of yourself; low because you do not feel you deserve care, and high because you think you get to decide that's true. Who are you to rob someone of fulfilling the law of Christ?

I am thankful to a friend who showed me how to think of this. While sharing with her a confusing and seemingly interminable burden in my life, I said, "I hope I am not burdening you too much." She smiled and replied, "I can pick up your burden today. And when I am too tired, I will set it down." Here, again, thinking about my struggles as a burden I (and my friends) could pick up and set down rather than an elusive heaviness that wafts from one person's veins to another's really helped me feel relieved. Even being able to set down my burden for a little while, to put it in the capable hands of another person, made me feel more ready to face life.

There is another way in which it helped. It made me realize that by setting down my burden, I could also look at it, sort through it, check and see if there was anything I needed to take out of the backpack of my life to make carrying it easier.

Sometimes, I think our hesitancy to let other people bear our burdens is that we confuse bearing each other's burdens with talking about them. Just because we speak to someone about what is heavy in our lives doesn't mean that they now need to carry that thing. Sometimes what friends offer is not to carry our burdens for us, but to look at our burdens with us, and to tell us, "It's okay. You don't need to carry that thing. You can throw it in the trash." They can help us do what I occasionally do when my work bag has been becoming increasingly heavy without my knowing exactly why—because I've been acquiring library books and things from the grocery store that I forgot to unload. Having a friend (or, in some more weighty cases, a therapist) look at your burdens with you, decide which ones can be neatly stored away, which ones can go all together, and which ones are just a part of the *weight of living* can be incredibly helpful. And yet it seems we are often resistant to showing other people our burdens. Why is this? How can we change?

## Taking a) Ourselves Lightly b) A Bath

One of the things that keeps us from unburdening ourselves is shame, the fear of becoming burdens ourselves. While many of the medicines for our maladies in life are bitter, one of the cures for shame is very sweet: laughter. In his study of shame, Gershen Kaufman writes that laughter and humor are "effective means of reducing intense negative affect, particularly shame."[3]

There is both an affective and an intellective component of humor: we *laugh* (affective) at a joke because we *get* (intellective) that joke. A joke helps us conceptualize our burdens (especially shame and fear) as burdens rather than heaviness; it makes these things something outside of ourselves that we can look at and poke fun at. And humor also tends to be communal; we tell a joke to someone else, and even if we laugh only to ourselves, there is an implied relationship between what we laugh at and ourselves. It is for this reason that twentieth-century theologian Reinhold Niebuhr describes humor as a "prelude" to faith, and one of the steps one can take on the road to repentance. He writes: "Humour is . . . a by-product of self-transcendence. People with a sense of humour do not take themselves too seriously. They are able to 'stand off' from themselves, see themselves in perspective, and recognize the ludicrous and absurd aspects of their pretensions."[4] Humor allows us to take the burden of shame out of ourselves, to set it on the ground and look at it with amusement.

You might be thinking, *I do not find my own shame amusing*, but here again humor can help us. Humor can help us see the relative unimportance and tininess of our own failings in true proportion to the rest of the world. Niebuhr describes this well and amusingly:

> When man surveys the world he seems to be the very center of it; and his mind appears to be the unifying power which makes sense out of the whole. But this same man, reduced to the limits of his animal existence, is a little animalcule, preserving a precarious moment of existence within the vastness of space and time. There is a profound incongruity between the "inner" and the "outer" world. . . . The incongruity becomes even more profound when it is considered that it is the same man who assumes the ultimate perspective from which he finds himself so insignificant.[5]

There is a comfort that comes with realizing we are simply not that big of a deal, that no matter what our failures or our embarrassments, they are nothing to the vast love of God. "What is funny about us," Niebuhr writes, "is precisely that we take ourselves too seriously. We are rather insignificant little bundles of energy and vitality in a vast organization of life."[6] Laughing at ourselves allows us to bring our burdens before God and before other people, so that we can think of how to lighten them and how to proceed. Of course, this can go too far; laughter, regarding ourselves with amusement and realizing our smallness, should lead us to *rest* in God, to throw ourselves on His mercy. Realizing our smallness is only comforting if it means we can depend on something greater than ourselves to rest in. Niebuhr writes: "There are ultimate incongruities of life which can be resolved by faith but not by reason. . . . They are also too profound to be resolved or dealt with by laughter. If laughter seeks to deal with the ultimate issues of life it turns into a bitter humour."[7]

G. K. Chesterton famously wrote, "Angels can fly because they can take themselves lightly,"[8] but there are other benefits to taking yourself lightly. When you realize your insignificance in the grand scheme of things, and particularly the "limits of . . . animal existence," you can take a more targeted and strategic approach to bearing your burdens. My tendency is to think that my burdens are very big, very existential, that they must be solved only by moving heaven and earth. Very often, they are solved by a snack, a nap, or a bath.

Thomas Aquinas, the plodding bull as he was called in his own century (the fifteenth), is one of the towering figures of Christian theology. His unfinished *Summa Theologica*, made up of 2,669 articles and around 1.8 million words, persists as one of the most important texts in theology and philosophy, seeming to have an answer for almost everything, from divine simplicity to arguments for God's existence. Personally, however, I am most affectionately attached to the article in which he explores the "remedies of sorrow" in which he concludes that sorrow might be assuaged by several things: friends, tears, the truth, and baths.[9] The last is my favorite.

Article five begins (as all the articles begin) with a question: "Whether pain and sorrow are assuaged by sleep and baths?" Aquinas takes his usual approach, first by enumerating objections to the idea that sleep and baths might assuage sorrow, then with a general thesis to the contrary, followed by a line-by-line reply to all the objections. The general theme of the objections (with differing intricacies of argument, of course) is that baths cure ailments of the body, where sorrow is a matter of the inner disposition of the heart (or, even, the soul). As his initial evidence winding up to the contrary arguments he quotes Augustine, who describes a bath that drives sadness from the mind; a hymn of Ambrose about the sorrow-assuaging power of naps; and the words of Epiphany vespers: "Sleep restores the tired limbs to labor, refreshes the weary mind, and banishes sorrow." His more substantial reply and argument buttressed for the benefits of baths is this: "Every good disposition of the body reacts somewhat on the heart, which is the beginning and end of bodily movements."[10] The movements of the heart and body are not so separate. We know this because of the bodily effects of sorrow (tears, stomach aching, difficulty sleeping). Why then can the opposite direction not also work? To soothe bodily pain can ease the heart too.

This brings me back to the words of Jesus: "I will give you rest" (Matthew 11:28). Part of the way we can learn to bear our burdens is by learning to set them down sometimes, to rest, to care for the symptoms they have created in us—the tired shoulders, the aching head, the weariness. Accepting the animal nature of our existence helps us take ourselves more lightly and helps us respond to our burdens in a more practical way. Often when we are feeling heavy, our temptation is to think our way out of the pain and confusion, when what we really need to do is take a nap and a bath.

## Pick Up Your Cross

The very language that Jesus uses to describe a life of discipleship is that of something we must pick up and carry: "Whoever wants to be my disciple must deny themselves and take up their cross and follow me" (Matthew 16:24). We will all bear burdens in life. The weight of living is not all bad. To carry the upbringing of a child, or the responsibility of a meaningful vocation, the lifelong vow to love another person, is a profound honor, but it requires a great deal of us and can feel heavy sometimes, almost too heavy. And we all also carry burdens that we did not choose—the metaphorical portable microphones that someone left in our office and we now find ourselves having to deal with. Life is not fair, and it is not equal; some of us bear more burdens than others, cast on us by traumatic experiences, loss, mental health issues, or the irresponsibility of others. We also carry the burdens of things we did choose, and regret: sin, bad decisions, faltering love. The quality of our lives will be shaped by the burdens we choose to carry, and the way that we carry them.

In Hebrews 11, after describing the worthy lives of many saints that have come before him, the author of Hebrews writes, "Therefore, since we are surrounded by such a great cloud of witnesses, let us throw off everything that hinders and the sin that so easily entangles. And let us run with perseverance the race marked out for us" (Hebrews 12:1). The author encourages us to get rid of burdens that slow us down from running the race, that is living the life, to which we are called. I know that a meaningful life will have burdens, but we are also told not to carry unnecessary burdens. A part of the everyday work of life is continually sorting through our knapsack and getting rid of what we cannot or should not carry, so that we carry only the easy yoke of Christ.

But even as we cast off the burdens that we ought not carry, we should cherish the guidance that burdens can offer us. To love someone is a weighty thing, and yet the burden of love may not be a mere obstacle to running the race of life; it can direct and orient our action as well, give us a direction of travel. To submit to the yoke of Christian love is to bear a weighty thing, but that weight is one which can orient us and guide us on the *path of life*, the final metaphor of this book.

## LIVING, THINKING, PRAYING

Whoever wants to be my disciple must deny themselves and take up their cross daily and follow me. For whoever wants to save their life will lose it, but whoever loses their life for me will save it. What good is it for someone to gain the whole world, and yet lose or forfeit their very self?

Luke 9:23–25

## ■ LIVING METAPHORS

Take a bath. When you drain the bath, stay in the tub as the water drains. Observe how your body feels as the water ceases to carry you, as you begin to bear the weight of your own body. What does the weight of your own life feel like? Can you bear it? What lifts the weight of your life like water?

## ■ THINKING AND PRAYING

*Poem:* "Harlem" (1951), Langston Hughes

*Book: The Pilgrim's Progress* (1678), John Bunyan

*Poem: The Rime of the Ancient Mariner* (1798), Samuel Taylor Coleridge

*Painting: Never Morning Wore to Evening but Some Heart Did Break* (1894), Walter Langley

*Music:* "American Tune," *The Concert in Central Park Live* (1982), Simon and Garfunkel

Langston Hughes' iconic poem describes disappointment—the deep, lifelong kind—in the language of metaphor. Disappointment is dried out, infected, rotten, sickly sweet, or heavy. I am struck by that simple line "Maybe it just sags." Hughes was a central figure in the Harlem Renaissance, a movement of poets, musicians, and writers who sought to cultivate an authentically Black expression of art and culture after the devastations of slavery in America. For those who moved north after the end of the Civil War, places like Harlem, New York, promised to be bastions of new freedom, self-expression, and creativity. But often, that hope was stifled, that dream, as the poem describes, deferred. The final line is interesting—does Hughes' metaphor of the exploding dream seem hopeful or destructive? How do these metaphors invite us to regard disappointment?

*Pilgrim's Progress* tells the story of a different kind of burden: guilt. In the allegorical telling of the Christian journey, the protagonist of *Pilgrim's Progress* sets out to be relieved of the great burden of his sins. Some characters help him bear his burden, and some add to its difficulties so that it nearly weighs him down altogether, until ultimately the straps of his burden break before the cross; here he learns that losing his burden is only the beginning of his Christian journey.

A sudden and miraculous lifting of the burden of guilt is also depicted in Samuel Taylor Coleridge's *The Rime of the Ancient Mariner*, in which, as a result of an inexplicably cruel act toward an innocent creature, the central character is made to carry an albatross (a very large bird) around his neck. Some commentators have suggested that the poem partially wrestles with Coleridge's own addiction to opium. It is only when he begins to receive life, even all the slimy creatures that beset his lost ship, as a gift that prayer comes to his lips unbidden, and the albatross falls from his neck. Both Bunyan's and Coleridge's works in their own way deal with the burdens that we both choose and do not choose, burdens of both sin and suffering, and most importantly, the burdens we cannot lift off ourselves.

Langley's painting compassionately portrays an older woman comforting a younger woman. As we look on the scene, we might wonder about the nature of the burden for which the younger woman seeks comfort. Is it a fresh grief over sudden bad news? Or is it exasperation from an old, habitual weariness—a burden born day in and day out for years on end? Her body language is that of someone carrying a burden: bent down, stooped, pulled by gravity. But here too we see someone in the act of bearing another person's burden. The old woman turns toward the young one in an act of attentive compassion, an unhurried presence to console her. Langley's title for the painting acknowledges the ubiquity of sorrow in the world, but the image also offers consolation in its depiction of solidarity.

It is this brotherhood of solidarity that Simon and Garfunkel evoke in both the lyrics and the musical references woven into their song. In contrast to the patriotic triumph you might expect from a song with the title "American Tune," the lyrics speak of the burdens of the everyday man or woman whose efforts seem never to be enough and whose consolations are few. The song borrows the bulk of its melody from Paul Gerhardt's "O Haupt voll Blut und Wunden" ("O Sacred Head, Now Wounded"), which plays a central role in Bach's St. Matthew Passion. It is an invitation to share in the sufferings of Christ, who, in His own sufferings, expresses solidarity with the suffering of mankind. In this nod to Bach, Simon evokes a sense of solidarity between burdened ordinary Americans, among all mankind, and perhaps even solidarity with God. In a chance to share in one another's suffering, we find that suffering relieved, easier to bear.

# LIFE
## IS (NOT)
# A JOURNEY

We have countless choices on our "life's journey." We can make detours and take byways; we can stand still; perhaps also we can, in a certain sense, go backward. Above all we can progress in the true direction. Only one alternative is barred to us, that of not being en route at all, of not being "on the way."

Josef Pieper, *Death and Immortality*

Jesus answered, "I am the way."

John 14:6

**W**hen I was nine years old, my mother encouraged me to memorize Robert Frost's poem "The Road Not Taken." I recited it in front of a ballroom filled with people. I wore ballet flats and did my best to project to the back of the room, as my mother and drama teacher advised. "Two roads diverged in a yellow wood," I began with a slightly wavering voice, but as the words came out of my mouth and filled the room, I picked up confidence. I *made my* way through the five lines of the four stanzas, *proceeding confidently* through its irregular iambic tetrameter, *not stumbling.* Just like the traveler in the poem, I completed my recitative expedition, arriving triumphantly at its conclusion:

> I took the one less traveled by,
> And that has made all the difference.[1]

I followed my performance with a little bow and was rewarded with the generous applause of an audience of mothers who were all encouragement and delight. Afterward people complimented me in the way that young girls are often complimented; I was poised, some told me (for what? attack?) and others that I had a good stage presence. I enjoyed the experience, but what would stay with me much longer than the gratification of performing well before a crowd of adoring adults (though I can't help but feel that left its mark as well) was the poem itself. As memorized things have a habit of doing, it etched itself onto the wallpaper of my mind. When, each October, my family would drive from our home in the foothills of the Rocky Mountains to higher altitudes for a glimpse of the golden cloak of aspens that adorned the sloping mountains, I would speak the words to myself when we parked to take a walk through a particularly resplendent patch of autumnal glory: "Two roads diverged in a yellow wood." And they did. It was a pleasure to feel the words making the golden forest somehow even more lovely to me, to have inside me fitting words for fitting moments.

Somewhere along the way the poem began to bring with it mists of anxiety. At seventeen I placed two college acceptance letters before me. *Sorry I could not travel both,* I opted for the place with the most sunshine and financial assistance. To be honest, I wasn't that sorry I couldn't travel both since one of the paths led to a cornfield in Indiana, but the phrase gave me some clarity anyway: here I was at the beginning of my life, making choices, taking a step down this path and not another.

Sometimes when I chatted on the phone with my mom, she would say, "Well, *knowing how way leads on to way* . . ." letting the sentence dangle, implying the shadow of many as yet unlived lives. Moments of real, weighty divergence began to present themselves, first here and there, and then at a frightening, rapid speed: which grad school to choose, whether to do a PhD, whether to take this job or that one, which country to live in, whether to marry (this man) or not. I hadn't stumbled over the poem all those years ago, but I feared I would stumble now. The roads diverged, and I, I hesitated.

I can't blame it all on Robert Frost, but I had absorbed a few ideas about the path of life that generated great anxiety in me and didn't always, I think, aid me in the choices I made. The first was that *the road less traveled* was always the *better path*, and so I should always choose the most difficult and challenging option. In its own way, the poem could be read as profoundly American; a good life is one forged through the powers of self-determination. We value the cowboy, the artist, the rugged individualist who strikes out on their own on a path that hasn't been cleared.

The second was a hazy sense that *way leading on to way* had a sort of concrete quality to it, like a choose-your-own-adventure video game, where once you follow this way, the choices you make are set in stone and, as the saying goes (appropriate to the metaphor), *you can never go back*.

And finally, I felt deep in my bones that, as the poem says, my choices *made all the difference*. This was empowering in a way, but could also be deeply crippling. You and I can choose which path we take; we are not entirely controlled by the caprice of fate. And yet, in this way of thinking, if things go poorly, it's *my fault*.

And so I proceeded for a long time, with a haze of uncertainty, but with determination, until one day, in a moment of rare clarity, I knew myself to be on the wrong path, or, at least, a path that would lead me somewhere I wasn't interested in going, toward becoming something I wasn't interested in becoming. I discovered that Christians must be absolutely committed to the idea of turning around. What would the story of the prodigal son be if having taken one path, we could not take another? I learned that life may be a journey, but journeys often involve *getting lost, backtracking,* accidentally taking a loop and ending up in the same place. I knew with great clarity that turning back was the right decision, but no other clear path presented itself. I turned from a bright path leading somewhere I didn't want to go, to a murky wood without a clear path forward. It was then that I found another poem began to ring more true to my experience:

> Midway upon the journey of our life
> I found myself within a forest dark,
> For the straightforward pathway had been lost.[2]

Like Dante in the "forest dark" I began to feel that the "straightforward pathway had been lost." Indeed, I myself began to *feel lost,* like I didn't know *which steps to take next.* I wanted God to send a messenger, a clear sign to *set me on the right path,* but instead all I got were loving and imperfect Virgils who walked beside me as we encountered sometimes disturbing and sometimes beautiful scenes. Gradually, though the "straightforward path" never became straightforward, I began to feel a growing momentum, that even though I was not sure where I was going, I was becoming a better traveler, more skilled, more resilient, more curious, more apt to suck the marrow out of the good in life. I began to speak less of the "forest dark" and more, as Dante puts it, of "the good . . . which there I found."[3] I began to think that the destination which I sought was always slightly out of reach and out of sight, that the task of life was taken up with attempts to journey faithfully, the companionship that drives us toward the unseen vistas, and the sources of rest we find along the way. These poems gave a life and vocabulary to a metaphor that was already thoroughly operative in my own life: *life is a journey*. This is the last metaphor this book will *explore*.

## The Path of Life

Writing this chapter has been very difficult. Why? It is because I haven't been sure what exactly I am talking about. *Life is (not) a journey*. I begin with the important words: life, journey. What is life? I begin my writing with this question. It should be simple, shouldn't it? Is life the principle of vitality, animation, that we see in animate creatures? Or is life *a life*, a span of time in which existence takes a particular form? Or is life something more extensive, more permeating? Is life the thing that undergirds all the things I'm trying to describe—the heart that beats, the grass that grows, perhaps even the rock that sits? With each answer I searchingly try on for size, I find myself more discomfited; I am in too deep, I am beyond my pay grade. What is life?

What is a journey? Here, I think I will find easier ground. After all, isn't this a part of the gift of metaphors? *You, love, sadness*—these are elusive concepts to pin down, too porous to keep within the borders of a definition, always leaking when you try. This is why we reach for metaphors, ways of speaking rooted in the things we can taste, touch, smell, to explain things that cannot be so easily defined. But here, too, I ran into trouble. What is a journey? Is a journey a path, the line you follow on a map? Is it the time spent on the journey, the expedition spanning from the early dawn of a day, through an unforgiving noon, arriving in the evening? Or the experiences you have along the path? What part do your companions play? Even as I ask these questions, I realize I am dangerously close to becoming a ridiculous inspirational plaque in a home-and-garden shop. Life is not about the destination, but the journey. But what is life and what is a journey? Here again, *I am lost.*

I think the difficulty of landing on a definition for either *journey* or *life* is that this metaphor encompasses much more than the other metaphors; within the journey of life, one can be in the *forest dark* (the way unknown, wisdom hidden), one can seek the *safety of a high place*, one can carry *the weight of living*, one can even think of birth itself as an *arrival*. While these other metaphors are in some sense concrete and discrete—tree, tower, birth—a journey itself is something like a concept, not a concrete object or process we can point to. It remains a metaphor since it is an experience most of us have had; most of us have a strong enough sense of a journey to carry its properties over to life. But the boundaries of its meaning are slippery, elusive; they grow and shrink, they can mean a lot or a little.

Life as a concept has a similar problem, and a similar capaciousness. Life itself can involve all of the ideas explored in this book—persons, love, safety, creation, burdens, thought—and, indeed, all these concepts necessarily involve life. Life is the precondition for love, for change, for safety. It seems to me that the reason it is so difficult to define *life* and to define *journey* is that they both encompass and undergird all that I have tried to describe in this book.

A property of the life that animates all these things is that it endures; life has duration, a temporal element, an ongoing impact on the world. All my efforts to love or be safe or to change happen in the circumference of life, *this* life, *my* life. And in the same way that life underpins all of the concepts this book has explored, the metaphor of journey ties together many of the metaphors in this book.

The idea of the *path of life* is a theme that runs throughout much of Scripture, particularly in wisdom literature. In fact, with a backward glance we can see that it runs through much of the imagery that we've already explored. The *path of life* is often portrayed in a mirror image: the path of the righteous contrasted with the path of the wicked, the path of the wise with the path of the fool. One of the fascinating things to me about this cluster of imagery is that it often intersects with the metaphors explored in this book: light and darkness as wisdom and foolishness, height as safety and depth as danger, and even trees as people.

When we explored Psalm 1 in the opening chapter, we pressed into its portrayal of *people as trees*, but the initial metaphor of the psalm is of *a person traveling*. The blessed person is one who comports himself in a particular way on the *path of life*, avoiding the *wicked way* of walking, *sinful paths*, and *mocking companions* (v. 1). This psalm presents us with a mixed metaphor; the righteous man is like a tree walking. It is reminiscent of J. R. R. Tolkien's ents, mythical creatures somewhere between trees and humans, their faces framed by leaves richly green, moving but still somehow rooted. Tolkien's imagined creatures bear witness to the similarities between trees and humans, a connection our minds can intuitively make.

It's a strange melding of the *path of life* imagery with *tree* imagery.

The interpolation of *path imagery* is everywhere in Scripture. Take, for example, light as wisdom: "The *path of the righteous* is like the morning sun, *shining ever brighter* till the full light of day. But *the way of the wicked* is like *deep darkness*; they do not know what makes them stumble" (Proverbs 4:18–19, italics added). It seems to me that the metaphor of light here is employed not as a metaphor on its own, but as an outworking of the *path of the righteous* metaphor. Wisdom illuminates the path before us, and the righteous man walks in it. God, and more specifically God's words, are a source of light, guiding us on the *path of life*, and so the psalmist finds himself praying and praising God that "Your word is a lamp for my feet, a light on my path" (Psalm 119:105). "Wisdom will save you from *the ways of wicked men*, from men whose words are perverse, who have left the *straight paths to walk in dark ways*" (Proverbs 2:12–13, italics added). The human person is on the move, traveling through the land of the living. Light is employed as a metaphor for wisdom because travelers on the road of life need light, and they need wisdom to know how to proceed. The metaphors of path and light intersect, just as the nature of life and wisdom are wound tightly together.

This is also true for the metaphor of *safety as height*. "It is God who arms me with strength and *keeps my way secure*. He makes my feet like the feet of a deer; he causes me to *stand on the heights*" (Psalm 18:32–33, italics added). The invocation of height presents God (or wisdom) acting as a guide for the righteous on the path of life. This overlaps with the metaphor of wisdom as light; the light of wisdom shows us which path to take, which is safe, what lies on the path, and where it leads. The safe path is upward, away from flooding and dark ravines, the "pit" as Proverbs and the Psalms often refer to it, and toward the mountaintop, where you can see a long way. Contrarily, the path of the wicked leads downward, toward danger and death. Solomon describes Folly as a woman whose "house *leads down to death* and *her paths to the spirits of the dead*" (Proverbs 2:18, italics added). Along the *path of life* we seek security, which is often to be found on paths that lead to high places. *Safety* and *life* are hand in hand.

In various ways the other metaphors in this book also interact with the path motif. "Whoever *walks with the wise* becomes wise, but *the companion of fools will suffer harm*" (Proverbs 13:20 ESV, italics added). Here we see a meditation on, if not love, companionship, those with whom we walk on *the path of life*. With those we love, we walk as companions. Companions keep us safe, encourage us on the path, sometimes even lead us astray, and can cause us to *suffer harm*, just as a bad love can be a sickness.

Birth, too, can be wedded to the metaphor of journey. Scripture often speaks of *bringing forth* a child; a change from interior to exterior, a journey from dark to light, from womb to world. Birth is the beginning of the *journey of life*, and parents are meant to guide the children they bring into it, to show them how to walk on the path of the righteous. To be born is to be *sent out* into the world on the *journey of life*, and this is reflected in the way that parenting is often described in terms of *teaching a child the ways of righteousness*.[4] In Deuteronomy God's actions toward Israel are likened to a parent's: "Know then in your heart that as a man disciplines his son, so the Lord your God disciplines you. Observe the commands of the Lord your God, *walking in obedience to him* and revering him" (Deuteronomy 8:5–6, italics added). A good parent teaches and disciplines their child, and good discipline shows children how to *walk in the ways of God*. In the second chapter of 1 John, the beloved disciple addresses the church as "dear children" five times, explaining that "everyone who does what is right has been *born of him*" (2:29, italics added) and warning the members of the church "about those who are trying to *lead you astray*" (v. 26, italics added). The message is clear: true children born of God walk in God's ways; follow them.

Drawing on the imagery of *life as a journey*, the author of Hebrews ups the ante by describing the Christian life as a *race*, writing, "Therefore, since we are surrounded by such a great cloud of witnesses, let us *throw off everything that hinders* and the *sin that so easily entangles*. And let us *run with perseverance the race marked out for us*" (Hebrews 12:1 italics added).

And on that race, we must consider what may hinder us, slow us down, namely *burdens*. The Psalms sometimes describe sin not only as that which leads us astray from the path of the righteous, but as that which loads us down with a burden of guilt that makes walking the path more difficult: "My guilt has overwhelmed me like *a burden too heavy to bear*" (Psalm 38:4, italics added). But there are other burdens too, burdens other than sin; 1 Peter encourages its readers to "Cast all your anxiety [or burdens] on him because he cares for you" (5:7), and Jesus says He will both give us rest and make our burdens light (Matthew 11:30).

Most poignantly and succinctly, Jesus himself describes the Christian life as a journey with a load to bear. He said, "If anyone would come after me, let him deny himself and *take up his cross* and follow me" (Matthew 16:24 ESV, italics added). The Christian life is the path to Golgotha, *bearing up* under the weight of the cross.

The way in which the motif of *path* or *way* overlaps with so many other metaphors suggests to me something about the nature of journeys: they encompass more than simply where you are going. The metaphors are drawn in to make sense of *how the righteous travel, who they associate with,* and *where they are going, what they carry.* Life is not one phenomenon among others, just as a journey is neither the path, nor the companions, nor the loads we bear. Life itself is the phenomenon that encompasses all other phenomena; the journey is the metaphor in which all other metaphors sit. In our common parlance, our poetry, and the pages of Scripture, *life as a journey* breathes as an expansive and pervasive metaphor for that expansive and pervasive category of life. It is no wonder, I suppose, that I have always felt rootless, when one of our most dominant metaphors for life is travel.

## Wayfarers

In the opening of this book, I wrote about my affinity for restless Saint Augustine, and here, I find myself returning to him. The metaphor he most frequently uses to describe the human condition is that of pilgrimage. For many of us, the word *pilgrimage* brings to mind a hazy scene of the origins of Thanksgiving, people in dark clothing with fetching hats. Or we might think of travelers on the Camino, of pendants and cathedrals, a journey taken for spiritual enrichment, or, more crassly, spiritual tourism.

St Andrews, Scotland, the little town where I spent the bulk of my twenties, was a medieval pilgrimage site, a place where the pious and the piteous came to say their prayers, to obtain their miraculous medals, to seek miracles or indulgences. The idea of life being a journey is one that smells slightly of sentimentality, but Augustine's use of *pilgrimage* has a more capacious meaning, and a more melancholy one. For Augustine, pilgrimage is less like tourism and more like exile, being a refugee. His use of the metaphor circles around different forms of the same word: "*peregrinatio* (the noun: sojourn, exile, journey), *peregrinari* (the verb: to sojourn, wander, travel), or *peregrinus* (the subject: the wayfarer, sojourner, exile, pilgrim)."[5] A pilgrim is one who is searching, who is not at home.

Pilgrimage, for Augustine, is less like the golden carpet of autumnal leaves in Robert Frost, and more like a long security line at the airport. "Let us not forget," writes Sarah Stewart-Kroeker, "that *molesta est peregrinatio*—the sojourn is tiresome. Travel in the ancient world was largely a misery. . . . Being conveyed along ancient roads in a cart or wagon was a jarring, bruising, and nausea-inducing experience. . . . Taking a trip meant facing the very real prospect of dying on the way."[6] Life is no picnic for Augustine, and she adds, "Augustine himself hated traveling."[7]

This is not to say that the metaphor is one that sees life as a mere vale of tears; the pilgrimage of life has its pleasures, chief among them the companions on the road with us. There is much that is valuable and good and adventurous on the journey of life for Augustine. There are treacherous paths to tread, moments of discomfort and danger. But there are also moments of triumph, friendship, and comfort along the way.

It is almost an inspiring image. But the multivalences of *peregrinatio* offer us a more somber view of life. Gillian Clark observes that "a *peregrinus* is not a pilgrim, a purposeful traveler in search of enlightenment, but is someone who feels foreign and wants to go home."[8] It is not merely that we are walking through life, but that we are seeking a destination that is always out of sight, a home we never reach. The melancholy in Augustine's writing is not merely that traveling can be difficult, dangerous, and uncomfortable, it is that we long for a home we are exiled from. We are homesick.

This theme of a painful longing is one that Augustine drew forth from his own life and could be characterized by what the German existentialists might call *Unheimlichkeit*, a radical homelessness. This homelessness is not only cultural or geographical, but spiritual and intellectual. In his *Confessions*, he journeys not only *outward* into the world, but *inward* to his own "internal geography." This search is carried out with a sort of desperate ache, an inability to be at home in the world, a desperate desire to find a way.

It should come as no surprise that Augustine's work haunts the work of the twentieth-century existentialists like Albert Camus (who wrote his thesis on Augustine) or the towering and problematic philosopher Martin Heidegger. This feeling of restlessness is where Heidegger begins his probing work on the nature of being. He writes,

> This is where we are driven in our homesickness: to being as a whole. Our very being is this restlessness. We have

somehow always already departed toward this whole, or better, we are always already on the way to it. But we are driven on, i.e., we are somehow simultaneously torn back by something, resting in a gravity that draws us downward. . . . What is the unrest of this "not"? We name it *finitude*.[9]

For Heidegger, philosophy begins with this gravitational pull along, this sense of lack and a desire to find something we've never had. We are caught in a Sisyphean dilemma, thrown into a world where we long for what we cannot rediscover. Restless, as Augustine famously puts, until we find our rest in God.[10]

But perhaps there is rest to be found. In *On the Road with Saint Augustine* (2019), James K. A. Smith reflects on the resonances between the searching and open approach of Augustine's writing and the aching un-homed-ness of the twentieth-century philosophers and spiritual homelessness of our own age. Like Heidegger and Camus and their like, Smith too is interested in the experience of homelessness, and much of his thought begins in its fresh and somehow orientating pain. And yet, as Smith writes, "Augustine will unapologetically suggest that you were made for God—that home is found beyond yourself, that Jesus is the way, that the cross is a raft in the storm-tossed sea that we call 'the world.'"[11]

Augustine described his own life and spiritual wonderings within the contours and arch of an allegorical interpretation of the Prodigal Son. Lost and far from home, profligate in his living and loving, he is slowly drawn back from the "far" country by the companion who both shows him the way and is Himself the way: Christ. Life is a journey, a

God both shows him the way in Christ, and is the point of arrival for whom he has so desperately longed. Augustine writes, "Wisdom herself . . . had given us an example of how to live, in no other mode than the human one . . . since she herself is our home, she also made herself for us into the way home."[12] In finding Christ, Augustine found *The Way*, the path he should take on his pilgrimage, and a foretaste of arrival in God; and yet, even in that discovery, home was still just out of sight. Here begins the Christian life.

A central tension, then, of Augustine's theology is how one is to live well in this world if one is destined for the next. This is so much the case that his theology has sometimes been criticized as otherworldly, unconcerned with the injustices and ambiguities of this life. But for Augustine, the pains and burdens that come with love in this life are to be taken seriously, and become orientating pulls of gravity for us. The weight of love that we feel for the homeland directs us. He writes:

> The weight's movement is not necessarily downwards, but to its appropriate position: fire tends to move upwards, a stone downwards. They are acted on by their respective weights; they seek their own place. . . . By your gift we are set on fire and carried upwards: we grow red hot and ascend. We climb "the ascents in our heart" (Psalm 83:6), and sing "the song of steps" (Psalm 119:1). Lit by your fire, your good fire, we grow red-hot and ascend, as we move upwards "to the peace of Jerusalem" (Psalm 121:6). "For I was glad when they said to me, let us go to the house of the Lord" (Psalm 121:1). There we will be brought to our place by a good will, so that we want nothing but to stay there forever.[13]

For Augustine, the weight of love has a paradoxical gravity; love is pictured as a burden that does not pull us *down*, and as a weight that draws us *up*. Like the purified love of the white horse in Plato's *Phaedrus*, the longing for home can direct our early lives. Living with, even stirring our ache of love for our final homeland, gives our journey in life direction and orientation. The desire for roots, the feeling of not being at home, and the great ache that comes with it are burdens that *ground* us in this life. Augustine's characterization of the Christian life as a *pilgrimage* does not alleviate the inconsolable ache for home; it integrates it. "My weight is my love," writes Augustine. "Wherever I am carried, my love is carrying me."[14] The very weight that he carries of love for the homeland he has not reached orients him toward that homeland, and shows him how to conduct himself in this mixed life.

## The Long Obedience

A little less than a year after sitting on my stoop and wishing for a place to put my roots, I returned to the Auld Grey Toon (Old Gray Town) to walk in my graduation ceremony. That year was a bumper crop of graduations, the past two summers cancelled because of strict lockdowns and concern over spreading disease as thousands of families flew in from all over the world. This made it a particularly joyful day—celebrating, at last, what had been a grueling few years, not only for those of us gnashing our teeth through the final death throes of our theses, but for everyone. It was good to have a reason to celebrate. And summer in Scotland is very nearly perfect, weather wise.

When the principal rose, settled her papers on the podium with her usual neat poise, and began to speak, I was ready for a pleasant but forgettable commendation of our accomplishments, but instead she began to speak about walking. Walking, she reminded us, was about all we could do during the lockdowns when we weren't legally allowed to go more than a few kilometers from our houses, not allowed to see anyone outside our "bubble," not able to sit in a coffee shop. Almost everyone I knew then regimentally walked every day, a small routine of sanity amidst the benumbing brown that life became in those uncounted days. The perambulating silhouette of a friend from the distance was a happy thing, a day of foul weather a deep disappointment.

We trudged through lockdown, she noted, just as we trudged through our studies. A walk, she proposed, or perhaps more aptly, a marathon, was a compelling metaphor for the effort it had taken to *reach the finish line* of our studies in the midst of a global pandemic. Not a quick sprint and then finished, but day-by-day endurance training for that final, grueling but triumphant run toward the end. And this ending, she reminded us, this arrival, was just the beginning of a greater journey: life!

As we processed out into the golden summer sunshine, the organ played the theme song to *Chariots of Fire*, a film that tells the story of the runner-turned-missionary Eric Liddell. The opening scene of the movie features a dozen or more runners on West Sands Beach in St Andrews. Walking out as a graduate to that song was silly. It was triumphant. I'll never forget it.

The day was a lovely paradox: an arrival and a setting out, the ending of one season, and the beginning of another.

It felt like a momentous occasion, yes, but also a repetition of that old pattern: the repetition that looked like progression but led to the same thing: moving, once again. A new chapter. A new house. A new year. And yet, I did not feel so melancholy as I once did. Something had taken root in me, I think. An ache I chose to live with.

I have always found the concluding chapters of *The Lord of the Rings* series deeply moving, and deeply sad. Unlike some stories, which end in the breathy elation of the defeat of evil, Tolkien's classic does not end with triumph. Just because a war is over doesn't mean the towns have not been torn to pieces, and Tolkien spends many pages telling us who ended up where, what happened, and how the gradual healing of the land began. While this brings me a certain satisfaction as a reader, Tolkien does not offer a happy ending. Indeed, there is a deep melancholy, a presiding sense of loss alongside the consolation of victory, that marks the conclusion of the series. Returning from the defeat of Sauron, Frodo confesses to Gandalf that the wounds he received from the Ring Wraiths will not heal:

> "Are you in pain, Frodo?" said Gandalf quietly as he rode by Frodo's side.
>
> "Well, yes I am," said Frodo. "It is my shoulder. The wound aches, and the memory of darkness is heavy on me. It was a year ago today."
>
> "Alas! there are some wounds that cannot be wholly cured," said Gandalf.[15]

*Are you in pain?* Surely this is the greatest defeat of all; the very hero whose devotion made possible the salvation of Middle Earth cannot live in the world he saved. Darkness is defeated for a moment but pulls the hero down with it. This passage has always struck me to the heart because it rings true. Even in the best lives, there is sometimes an ache that we can't get rid of. And perhaps this is not such a bad thing. At the closing of the book, Frodo goes to the grey havens, a land within Middle Earth yet inaccessible to mortals, analogous to a good death. It is at this end where the reader catches a glimpse of at-home-ness:

> Then Frodo kissed Merry and Pippin, and last of all Sam, and went aboard. . . . And then it seemed to him that as in his dream in the house of Bombadil, the grey rain-curtain turned all to silver glass and was rolled back, and he beheld white shores and beyond them a far green country under a swift sunrise.[16]

Under this swift sunrise, the reader catches a whiff of paradise, of home, an ending to the pilgrimage. Frodo passing into a land associated and analogous with death could seem like the final defeat, and yet it is here that the reader detects the most permanent joyful turn in the story. Though every other good turn in the story is predicated upon an impermanent state of joy, waiting only for the next peril or enemy to defeat, this vision of bliss offers the final possibility of wholeness.

The Return of the King does not end with the raptures of Frodo but the commonness of Sam. Sam is not allowed the last view, the final consolation. The reader catches only a glimpse of Frodo's bliss, and then the story ends with the prosaic romance of ordinary life: Sam balances his daughter on his knee, draws a deep breath, and says, "Well, I'm back."[17] And so that is where this book, too, will end: at the beginning.

Sam, who in my mind is one of the true heroes of *The Lord of the Rings*, is given perhaps the most difficult task of all: to inhabit a world that has been wounded by war, and to make a home of the world in which he no longer fully belongs. It is not, you might think, so terrible a task; he has his good wife, Rosie, and their sweet children, a place he really can call home more than most of the rest of us can call our own place of origin home. And yet, having glimpsed the shores of the grey haven, and knowing that many of the people he loves best are there, this task of home-making is a bittersweet one. He must always be like a tree, rooted in the ground of the earthly home to which he's called, nourishing those around him, reaching upward, onward, homeward. Sam's life is like the Christian life that Augustine describes: home-making in a world that cannot be home to us.

When you think about it, home itself is a metaphor. I feel *at home* with you. She's *at home* in this field of study. We have all had homes, at one point or another, places where we not only lived, but felt particularly comfortable in, attached to, formed by. But like a journey and like life, the nature of home and its properties is an elusive thing. We can live in a house our whole lives and never feel at home in it, while one night in the walls of a place we've never been before can make us feel we finally belong. What makes a place a home seems to be some quality not in the home itself, not the walls, the door, even the hearth. What makes a house a home are properties that are not proper to the house, that are not intrinsic. It is some essential at-homeness that makes a house a home.

When we speak of earthly homes, then, it seems they are metaphors for another, more permanent home, a home whose qualities we borrow from in describing our earthly homes. Our heavenly home invites us to carry over its properties into these places in which we live. Insomuch as our houses are homes, they are metaphors for that true country we seek, carrying over the properties of the place to which our souls truly belong. In finding ways to be at home in the world, our lives become a metaphor of that true home. We become trees, rooted in the ground, reaching for our final home.

And perhaps in this way, all of the Christian life must be a metaphor. Preparing to make His journey to the cross, Jesus prayed for His disciples, saying, "I have given them your word and the world has hated them, *for they are not of the world any more than I am of the world.* My prayer is not that you take them out of the world but that you protect them from the evil one" (John 17:14–15, italics added). We are not to be taken out of this world, but to live intermingling our lives with our heavenly home. Just as our earthly homes themselves carry over their properties from that True Home, metaphorically speaking the form our life should take draws its shape from a more fundamental pattern. "Do not conform to the pattern of this world, but be transformed by the renewing of your mind," writes the apostle Paul (Romans 12:2). The Christian life itself is a metaphor, the carrying over of our true home to this world, where roots draw their nourishment from the springs of eternal life, unfolding in the light of True Wisdom, safe in the arms of the Most High, at home in love, changed from glory to glory, burdened only with the weight of love.

> Anyone who is still on pilgrimage, walking by faith, has not yet reached home but is already on the way to it. . . . Let us walk, then, like people who know they are on the way, because the king of our homeland has made himself our way. The king is the Lord Jesus Christ; there at home he is our truth, but here he is our way. To what are we traveling? To the truth. How shall we get there? Through faith. Whither are we traveling? To Christ. How shall we reach him? Through Christ. He told us himself, *I am the way, the truth and the life* (John 14:6).[18]

 ## LIVING, THINKING, PRAYING

> You will go out in joy and be led forth in peace; the mountains and hills will burst into song before you, and all the trees of the field will clap their hands.
>
> Isaiah 55:12

### ■ LIVING METAPHORS

Think of the longest trip you've taken—how long were you away from home? How was that trip? Did you find it invigorating and adventurous? Or draining or disorienting? What helped you to endure the long trip? What made it enjoyable? What do you wish you had done differently on this trip? Might this give you a way to think about your life at the moment?

## ▮ THINKING AND PRAYING

*Stories:* The Odyssey, Homer; *The Divine Comedy,* Dante
   Alighieri; *The Lord of the Rings,* J. R. R. Tolkien
*Music:* American folk tune "Wayfaring Stranger"
*Image: The Return of the Prodigal Son* (1669),
   Rembrandt

Each of these works of art evokes and explores the
themes of journeying, exile, and homecoming. The three
fictional epics, each composed in very different eras, all
center around a simple narrative: someone going somewhere. The entirety of Homer's *Odyssey* is about a man
trying to travel home to the person he loves. Dante's great
poem centers around the poet's journey through hell, purgatory, and heaven drawn on by his love of Beatrice, which
is transfigured and purified, so that Beatrice becomes the
source of desire that draws him toward God. The theme of
home and our personal relationships helping us in excru-
ciating journeys is at the heart of *The Lord of the Rings,* in
which numerous characters are sustained on their journey
by the memory of home. In these stories we are reminded
that often, in this life of exile, it is people in whom we find
home, and who call us into the journey of growth.

"Wayfaring Stranger" is an American folk tune, first re-
corded in a Christian songbook in 1858. It speaks of life
as a "Land of Woe," evoking that sense of *Unheimlichkeit*
that propels the singer on his journey. One imagines the
singer singing this to himself as he travels, exiled from home,
mother, and father, as both a comfort and an evocation of
his desire for a heavenly home.

Homecoming is the theme of Rembrandt's *Return of the Prodigal Son*. After a period of serious moral failing in his own life, which resulted in deep personal loss, Rembrandt portrays himself as the prodigal son in this painting. The father's hands, one feminine and one masculine, represent the gentle forgiveness and reconciliation of God, that true homecoming Rembrandt desired, the homecoming of the soul to its origin in God.

# EPILOGUE

## Plentiful Imagery

In this book, I have explored seven metaphors that I find in Scripture and in the world. Writing about them has been a rich and rewarding experience, and I hope a little bit of that pleasure has been passed on to you, my reader. But I hope also that as you close the pages of this book, you will find your appetite whetted rather than satiated for meditation on what Billy Collins playfully describes as the "plentiful imagery of the world,"[1] the ways in which our everyday experiences, when we pay attention to them, offer to us ways of thinking, praying, and living. Writing this has encouraged me to continue in that habit of attention to the world, and I hope it might have done the same for you, that you will pay attention to the world, its imagery, and its properties, and in so doing you will find, as Elizabeth Barrett Browning puts it, that

Earth's crammed with heaven,
And every common bush afire with God;
But only he who sees, takes off his shoes,
The rest sit round it and pluck blackberries.[2]

# FURTHER READING

## Introduction: Muddying the Waters

Aristotle. "Poetics, 1457b," *Aristotle in 23 Volumes, Vol. 23*, translated by W. H. Fyfe. Cambridge: Harvard University Press, 1932.

Aquinas, Thomas. *Summa Theologia* part I, question 13, article 3. New Advent.

Burns, Robert. "A Red, Red Rose" in *A Book of Scottish Song*, edited by Alexander Whitelaw. Glasgow: Blackie and Son, 1843.

cummings, e.e. "i thank You God for most this amazing day," *Selected Poems by e.e. cummings*, edited by Richard S. Kennedy. New York: Liveright, 1994.

Julian of Norwich. *Revelations of Divine Love*, translated by Grace Warrack. London: Methuen and Company, 1901.

Ricoeur, Paul. *The Rule of Metaphor*. London: Routledge, 1990.

Stewart-Kroeker, Sarah. *Pilgrimage as Moral and Aesthetic Formation in Augustine's Thought*. Oxford: Oxford University Press, 2017.

## Chapter 1: People are (not) Trees

Jamison, Henry. "I Forget Myself" featuring Darlingside. Color Study: 2020.

Swanton, Michael. "The Dream of the Rood," translated by Bond West. Exeter Medieval Texts and Studies. Liverpool: Liverpool University Press, 1996.

Williams, Rowan. *On Augustine*. London: Bloomsbury, 2016.

Wohlleben, Peter. *The Hidden Life of Trees: What They Feel, How They Communicate: Discoveries from a Secret World*, translated by Jane Billinghurst. Vancouver: Greystone Books, 2016.

Wong Kar-Wai, director. *In the Mood for Love*. Paradis Films, 2000, 98 minutes.

## Chapter 2: Wisdom is (not) Light

Aquinas, Thomas. "Scholars Prayer" in Wyatt North, Catholic Saints Prayer Book. Boston: Wyatt North Publishing, 2020.

Augustine, *Divine Illumination*, 5, from *Soliloquia 1.8.15*, translated by Thomas F. Gilligan in *The Fathers of the Church*, vol. 5. Washington, DC: Catholic University of America Press, 2008.

Barfield, Owen. *Saving the Appearances: A Study in Idolatry*. Middleton, CT: Wesleyan University Press, 1965, 1988.

Chesterton, G. K. *Orthodoxy*. New York: John Lane, 1908.

Kimbriel, Samuel. *Friendship as Sacred Knowing: Overcoming Isolation*. Oxford: Oxford University Press, 2014.

Milton, John. "Sonnet 19" *Milton's Sonnets*, edited by Mark Pattison. London: Kegan Paul, Trench, Trubner & Company, 1892.

Schumacher, Lydia. *Divine Illumination: The History and Future of Augustine's Theory of Knowledge*. Hoboken: Wiley, 2011.

Spektor, Regina. "The Light" track 6 on *Remember Us to Life*. Warner Brothers, 2016.

## Chapter 3: Safety is (not) a Fortress

Augustine. Sermon 87 on the New Testament, New Advent, www.newadvent.org/fathers/160387.htm.

Julian of Norwich. *Revelations of Divine Love*, translated by Grace Warrack. London: Methuen and Company, 1901.

Dante Alighieri. *The Divine Comedy*, translated by Henry Wadsworth Longfellow. Boston: Ticknor and Fields, 1867.

Ferrante, Elena. *Those Who Leave and Those Who Stay*, translated by Ann Goldstein. New York: Europa.

Lakoff, George and Johnson, Mark. *Metaphors We Live By*. Chicago: University of Chicago Press, 2003.

## Chapter 4: Love is (not) a Disease

Berry, Wendell. *Hannah Coulter.* Berkeley: Counterpoint, 2006.

Eliot, George. *Silas Marner.* New York: Signet Classics, 2007.

Healy, Matty, Daniel, George, and DJ Sabrina the Teenage DJ. "Happiness." Track two of *Being Funny in a Foreign Language.* London: Dirty Hit, 2022.

Lewis, C. S. *The Four Loves.* London: Geoffrey Bles, 1960.

Plato. *The Symposium and the Phaedrus,* translated by William S. Cobb. Albany, NY: State University of New York Press, 1991.

Teresa of Avila. *The Interior Castle,* translated by Rev. John Dalton. London: T. Jones, 1852.

## Chapter 5: Creation is (not) Birth

Arnalds, Ólafur. "Undone", track ten, *some kind of peace.* London: Decca Music, 2020.

Bergmann, Claudia. *Childbirth as a Metaphor for Crisis: Evidence from the Ancient Near East, the Hebrew Bible, and 1QH XI, 1–18.* Berlin: De Gruyter, 2008.

Carlisle, Clare. *The Marriage Question.* London: Allen Lane, 2023.

L'Engle, Madeleine. *Walking on Water: Reflections on Faith and Art.* Colorado Springs: Waterbrook Press, 1980.

MacIntyre, Alasdair. *Three Rival Versions of Moral Inquiry: Encyclopaedia, Genealogy and Tradition.* London: Bloomsbury Academic, 1990.

Nietzsche, Friedrich. *On the Genealogy of Morals,* translated by Douglas Smith. Oxford: Oxford University Press, 2008.

Plath, Sylvia. *Sylvia Plath: Collected Poems.* London: Faber & Faber, 2015.

Weston, L. M. C. "Women's Medicine, Women's Magic: The Old English Metrical Childbirth Charms," *Modern Philology,* Feb. 1995, Vol. 92, No. 3 (Feb. 1995), 279–293.

## Chapter 6: Sadness is (not) Heavy

Cloud, Henry and Townsend, John. *Boundaries: When to Say Yes, How to Say No, To Take Control of Your Life.* New York: Harper Collins, 2018.

Cloud, Henry and Townsend, John. *Safe People: How to Find Relationships That are Good for You and Avoid Those That Aren't.* Grand Rapids: Zondervan, 2016.

Kaufman, Gershen. *The Psychology of Shame.* New York: Springer Publishing Company, 1989.

Niebuhr, Reinhold. *Discerning the Signs of the Times.* London: Bloomsbury, 1946.

van der Kolk, Bessel. *The Body Keeps the Score: Brain, Mind, and Body in the Healing of Trauma.* New York: Penguin, 2014.

## Chapter 7: Life is (not) a Journey

Augustine. *Confessions,* translated by Henry Chadwick. Oxford: Oxford University Press, 1991.

Augustine. *Enarrationes in Psalmos,* 123.2, in Expositions of the Psalms, Vol. 6, edited by Boniface Ramsey, translated by Maria Boulding. Hyde Park, NY: New City Press, 2004.

Clarkson, Clay. *Heartfelt Discipline: Following God's Path of Life to the Heart of Your Child.* Monument, CO: Wholeheart Press, 2014.

Dante Alighieri, *The Divine Comedy,* translated by Henry Wadsworth Longfellow. Boston: Ticknor and Fields, 1867.

Frost, Robert. *Collected Poems of Robert Frost.* London: Longman's Green, 1939.

Heidegger, Martin. *The Fundamental Concepts of Metaphysics,* translated by William McNeill and Nicolas Walker. Bloomington, IN: Indiana University Press, 1983.

Smith, James K. A. *On the Road with Saint Augustine: A Real-World Spirituality for Restless Souls.* Grand Rapids, MI: Brazos Press, 2019.

Tolkien, J. R. R. *The Return of the King.* London: Harper Collins, 1998.

# NOTES

## Introduction

1. "William Morris Fabrics and Textiles," William Morris, william-morris.com/fabric.

2. Robert Burns, "A Red, Red Rose" in *A Book of Scottish Song*, ed. Alexander Whitelaw (Glasgow: Blackie and Son, 1843), 35.

3. Billy Collins, "Litany," in *Nine Horses* (London: Pan MacMillan, 2002), 70.

4. Aristotle, "Poetics, 1457b," *Aristotle in 23 Volumes*, Vol. 23, trans. W. H. Fyfe (Cambridge: Harvard University Press, 1932).

5. Paul Ricoeur, *The Rule of Metaphor* (London: Routledge, 1990), 292–293.

6. e.e. cummings, "i thank You God for most this amazing day," *Selected Poems by e.e. cummings*, ed. Richard S. Kennedy (New York: Liveright, 1994), 167.

7. Julian of Norwich, *Revelations of Divine Love*, trans. Grace Warrack (London: Methuen and Company, 1901), 149–150.

8. Thomas Aquinas, *Summa Theologia* part I, question 13, article 3, New Advent, www.newadvent.org/summa/1013.htm#article3.

9. Augustine, *Confessions*, trans. Henry Chadwick (Oxford: Oxford University Press, 1991), 3.

10. Sarah Stewart-Kroeker, *Pilgrimage as Moral and Aesthetic Formation in Augustine's Thought* (Oxford: Oxford University Press, 2017), 2.

## Chapter 1 People are (not) Trees

1. Michael Swanton, "The Dream of the Rood" (Liverpool: Liverpool University Press, 1996), 97. Translation by Bond West, who adds the following commentary on the first two lines: "These lines are hypermetric. By drawing out the normal metrical pattern of Germanic half-lines, the poet is presumably trying to heighten the sense of our Lord's torture being drawn out. It returns to standard metre once Jesus has given up His spirt. I can't really approximate this."

2. Oklahoma City National Memorial Museum, "The Memorial," https://memorialmuseum.com/experience/the-memorial.

3. Wong Kar-Wai, dir., *In the Mood for Love* (Paradis Films, 2000), 98 minutes.

4. Rowan Williams, *On Augustine* (London: Bloomsbury, 2016), 2–3.

5. Henry Jamison, "I Forget Myself," Single, Color Study/Ultra Records, 2020.

6. Peter Wohlleben, *The Hidden Life of Trees*, trans. Jane Billinghurst (Vancouver: Greystone Books 2016), 4.

## Chapter 2 Wisdom is (not) Light

1. Owen Barfield, *Saving the Appearances* (Middleton, CT: Wesleyan University Press, 1965, 1988), 116.

2. Augustine, *Divine Illumination*, 5, from *Soliloquia 1.8.15*, trans. Thomas F. Gilligan in *The Fathers of the Church*, vol. 5 (Washington, DC: Catholic University of America Press, 2008), 361–362.

3. Lydia Schumacher, *Divine Illumination: The History and Future of Augustine's Theory of Knowledge* (Hoboken: Wiley, 2011), 58–59.

4. Samuel Kimbriel, *Friendship as Sacred Knowing: Overcoming Isolation* (Oxford: Oxford University Press, 2014), 91.

5. Samuel Kimbriel, *Friendship as Sacred Knowing*, 92.

6. Thomas Aquinas, "Scholar's Prayer" in Wyatt North, Catholic Saints Prayer Book (Boston: Wyatt North Publishing, 2020).

7. G. K. Chesterton, *Orthodoxy* (New York: John Lane, 1908), 34.

8. John Milton, "Sonnet 19," *Milton's Sonnets*, ed. Mark Pattison (London: Kegan Paul, Trench, Trubner & Company, 1892).

9. John Milton, "Sonnet 19."

10. John Milton, "Sonnet 19."

11. "Canticle" in Morning Prayer, Northumbria Community, www.northumbriacommunity.org/offices/morning-prayer.

12. Antony Gormley, *Blind Light*, Hayward Gallery, 2007, www.ant onygormley.com/works/making/blind-light.

13. Regina Spektor, "The Light," track 6 on *Remember Us to Life* (Warner Brothers, 2016).

## Chapter 3 Safety is (not) a Fortress

1. George Lakoff and Mark Johnson, *Metaphors We Live By* (Chicago: University of Chicago Press, 2003), 14.

2. Augustine, "Sermon 87 on the New Testament," New Advent, www.newadvent.org/fathers/160387.htm.

3. Elena Ferrante, *Those Who Leave and Those Who Stay*, trans. Ann Goldstein (New York: Europa, 2014), 183.

4. Julian of Norwich, *Revelations of Divine Love*, translated by Grace Warrack (London: Methuen and Company, 1901), 198.

5. Diplo, Beyoncé, Henry Allen, Timothy Thomas, Theron Thomas, Ilsey Juber, Akil King, Jaramye Daniels, André Benjamin, Antwan Patton, Patrick Brown, "All Night," track 11 on *Lemonade* (Parkwood, 2016).

## Chapter 4 Love is (not) a Disease

1. Plato, *The Complete Works*, trans. Benjamin Jowett (Mineola, NY: Dover Thrift Editions, 2012), 163–165, italics added.

2. Plato, *The Complete Works*, 163–165.

3. Plato, *The Symposium and the Phaedrus*, trans William S. Cobb (Albany, NY: State University of New York Press, 1993), 102.

4. George Eliot, *Silas Marner* (New York: Signet Classics, 2007), 143–144.

5. Wendell Berry, *Hannah Coulter* (Berkeley: Counterpoint, 2006), 110.

6. Wendell Berry, *Hannah Coulter*, 109.

7. Wendell Berry, *Hannah Coulter*, 109.

8. Teresa of Avila, *The Interior Castle*, trans. Rev. John Dalton (London: T. Jones, 1852), 2.

9. George Daniel, Matthew Healy, and DJ Sabrina the Teenage DJ, "Happiness," track 2 on The 1975, *Being Funny in a Foreign Language* (London: Dirty Hit, 2022).

10. Ross MacDonald, George Daniel, Adam Hann, and Matthew Healy, "Sincerity Is Scary," track 6 on The 1975, *A Brief Inquiry into Online Relationships* (London: Polydor Records and Dirty Hit, 2018).

11. Ross MacDonald, Matthew Healy, George Daniel, and Adam Hann, "If I Believe You," track 6 on The 1975, *I Like It When You Sleep, For You Are So Beautiful Yet So Unaware of It* (London: Dirty Hit and Interscope Records, 2016).

12. William Blake, *The Marriage of Heaven and Hell* (Mineola, NY: Dover Publications, 1994), 31.

## Chapter 5  Creation is (not) Birth

1. Quoted and translated into English by L. M. C. Weston, "Women's Medicine, Women's Magic: The Old English Metrical Childbirth Charms," *Modern Philology* 92, no. 3 (1995), 292, www.jstor.org/stable /438781.

2. Some famous examples of this approach include Friedrich Nietzsche, *On the Genealogy of Morals,* trans. Douglas Smith (Oxford: Oxford University Press, 2008) and Alasdair MacIntyre, *Three Rival Versions of Moral Enquiry: Encyclopaedia, Genealogy, and Tradition* (London: Bloomsbury Academic, 1990).

3. Madeleine L'Engle, *Walking on Water: Reflections on Faith and Art* (New York: Convergent Books, 2001), 8.

4. Denise Levertov, "Annunciation" in *A Door in the Hive* (New York: New Directions Publishing, 1990), 86–88.

5. Denise Levertov, "Annunciation," in *A Door in the Hive,* 87.

6. Sylvia Plath, "Metaphors," *Sylvia Plath: Collected Poems* (London: Faber & Faber, 2015), 116.

7. Claudia Bergmann, *Childbirth as a Metaphor for Crisis: Evidence from the Ancient Near East, the Hebrew Bible, and 1QH XI, 1–18* (Berlin: De Gruyter, 2008).

8. Ólafur Arnalds, "Undone," track ten, *some kind of peace* (London: Decca Music, 2020).

9. The Form of Solemnization of Matrimony, *The Book of Common Prayer,* www.churchofengland.org/prayer-and-worship/worship-texts -and-resources/book-common-prayer/form-solemnization-matrimony.

10. Denise Levertov, "Annunciation," in *A Door in the Hive,* 88.

## Chapter 6  Sadness is (not) Heavy

1. Bessel van der Kolk, *The Body Keeps the Score: Brain, Mind, and Body in the Healing of Trauma* (New York: Penguin, 2014).

2. This idea is drawn from Henry Cloud and John Townsend, *Boundaries: When to Say Yes, How to Say No, To Take Control of Your Life* (New

York: Harper Collins, 2018), which is a good resource for thinking through how to think about other people's burdens. By the same authors, I'd also recommend *Safe People: How to Find Relationships That Are Good for You and Avoid Those That Aren't* (Grand Rapids: Zondervan, 2016), which explores how much we need each other, and how to both find and be a person who bears other people's burdens in a healthy and Christian way.

3. Gershen Kaufman, *The Psychology of Shame, Second Edition* (New York: Springer, 1996), 99.

4. Reinhold Niebuhr, *Discerning the Signs of the Times* (London: Bloomsbury, 1946), 106.

5. Reinhold Niebuhr, *Discerning the Signs of the Times*, 101.

6. Reinhold Niebuhr, *Discerning the Signs of the Times*, 106.

7. Reinhold Niebuhr, *Discerning the Signs of the Times*, 102.

8. G. K. Chesterton and Trevin Wax, *Orthodoxy: With Annotations and Guided Reading by Trevin Wax* (Nashville: B&H Academic, 2022), 172.

9. Thomas Aquinas, *Summa Theologiae*, I-II, Question 38, Article 5, *The Summa Theologiæ of St. Thomas Aquinas*, second and revised ed., 1920 New Advent. www.newadvent.org/summa/2038.htm#article5.

10. Thomas Aquinas, *Summa Theologiae*, I-II, Question 38, Article 5.

## Chapter 7 Life is (not) a Journey

1. Robert Frost, *Collected Poems of Robert Frost* (New York: Chartwell Books, 2016), 133.

2. Dante Alighieri, *The Divine Comedy*, trans. Henry Wadsworth Longfellow (Boston: Ticknor and Fields, 1867), 1.

3. Dante Alighieri, *The Divine Comedy*, 1.

4. See Clay Clarkson, *Heartfelt Discipline: Following God's Path of Life to the Heart of Your Child* (Monument, CO: Whole Heart Press, 2014).

5. Sarah Stewart-Kroeker, *Pilgrimage as Moral and Aesthetic Formation in Augustine's Thought* (Oxford: Oxford University Press, 2017), 10.

6. Sarah Stewart-Kroeker, *Pilgrimage as Moral and Aesthetic Formation*, 4.

7. Sarah Stewart-Kroeker, *Pilgrimage as Moral and Aesthetic Formation*, 12.

8. Gillian Clark, "Pilgrims and Foreigners: Augustine on Travelling Home," in *Travel, Communication and Geography in Late Antiquity*, eds. Linda Ellis and Frank L. Kidner (San Francisco: Ashgate, 2004), 149.

9. Martin Heidegger, *The Fundamental Concepts of Metaphysics,* trans. William McNeill and Nicholas Walker (Bloomington, IN: Indiana University Press, 1995), 5–6.

10. Augustine, *Confessions,* trans. Henry Chadwick (Oxford: Oxford University Press, 1991), 3.

11. James K. A. Smith, *On the Road with Saint Augustine: A Real-World Spirituality for Restless Souls* (Grand Rapids, MI: Brazos, 2019), xii.

12. Augustine, *Teaching Christianity,* trans. Edmund Hill (Hyde Park, NY: New City Press, 1996), 110–111.

13. Augustine, *Confessions,* 278–279.

14. Augustine, *Confessions,* 278.

15. J. R. R. Tolkien, *The Return of the King* (London: Harper Collins, 1998), 321.

16. Tolkien, *The Return of the King,* 377–378.

17. Tolkien, *The Return of the King,* 378.

18. Augustine, *Enarrationes in Psalmos,* 123.2, in *Expositions of the Psalms* Vol. 6, ed. Boniface Ramsey, trans. Maria Boulding (Hyde Park, NY: New City Press, 2004), 44.

## Epilogue

1. Billy Collins, "Litany," *Nine Horses* (London: Pan MacMillan, 2002), 70.

2. Elizabeth Barrett Browning, *Aurora Leigh* (Oxford: Oxford University Press, 2008), 246.